CAM TAIT

CAM TAIT & JIM TAYLOR

CAM TAIT

Disabled? HELL NO! I'm a Sit-Down Comic!

HARBOUR PUBLISHING

Harbour Publishing Co. Ltd.
P.O. Box 219, Madeira Park, BC, V0N 2H0
www.harbourpublishing.com

Edited by Patricia Wolfe
Text design Mary White
Cover design by Anna Comfort O'Keeffe
All photos courtesy of the Tait family unless otherwise noted
Front cover photo courtesy of Tom Braid
Printed in Canada

Harbour Publishing acknowledges the support of the Canada Council for the Arts, which last year invested $157 million to bring the arts to Canadians throughout the country. We also gratefully acknowledge financial support from the Government of Canada through the Canada Book Fund and from the Province of British Columbia through the BC Arts Council and the Book Publishing Tax Credit.

Cataloguing data available from Library and Archives Canada
ISBN 978-1-55017-697-1 (paper)
ISBN 978-1-55017-698-8 (ebook)

To Mom and Dad for giving me a dream,
and to my wife Joan, son Darren and grandson Nicholas
for taking me to new heights

Contents

foreword

My favourite Cam Tait story?

We're at the checkout counter of a posh downtown Vancouver hotel, Cam in his wheelchair, as the clerk processes his credit card and produces his bill. She is smiling and courteous, but as she places the bill on the counter she looks not at Cam, but at me.

"Does he sign his own name?" she asks.

"Migawd, Jim," Cam cries. "I'm deaf, too!"

He wasn't angry or upset at what obviously was an innocent slip-up. The line popped out because he has that kind of mind. It struck him as funny, and he let fly, because that's who he is.

In the twenty-five years I've known him, I've heard Cam laugh a lot, often at himself. I've heard him swear, I've heard him put down an athlete for what he sees as lack of maximum effort. But never, not even once, have I heard him whine. If he has railed against the fates that gave him cerebral palsy and sentenced him to life in a wheelchair—as logic says he must have—it's been done in private. Then, like his friend Rick Hansen, he hunkers down and gets on with his lifelong marathon.

What follows is an amazing story, full of dedicated people who rallied around two even more amazing parents and a baby who was born fighting for life and never learned to quit. You may choke up a bit, or lean over the bed to give your kids an extra hug. But you will come away smiling because, against all odds, it is a happy story of a life well lived, and growing happier by the day.

Enjoy.

—JIM TAYLOR

Prologue

"Nic," I said. "Let's go really slowly and take our time."

My grandson's small hands locked on to my knees and he paused for a second to secure his balance. I slowly rolled my wheelchair backwards with my feet. Nicholas was almost two years old at the time and was just learning how to walk. He kept a tight grip on my knees, then took one tentative step forward. Then another. I wheeled back a little more. Nicholas took another step. We repeated the process. And before we knew it, we were halfway across the living room floor. Nicholas' big brown eyes twinkled like I had never seen before, and he let out a genuine laugh.

A huge lump formed in my throat. I could not believe what was happening. I was helping my grandson learn how to walk—I, who had rarely walked alone and unaided in my life and needed years of relentless therapy to reach the point where I could take a few tottering steps.

When you have a physical disability, you are not often put in positions of trust. You grow up with people reminding you all the time that it's you who needs help, so how could you ever help others? The danger is that you may come to believe it.

Lack of oxygen at birth caused me to have cerebral palsy, meaning a part of my brain was damaged. I have used a wheelchair all my life, my arm and hand coordination isn't that great, and at times I can be difficult to understand. Yet, through the kindness and sacrifice of hundreds of people, there I was, joyously being not only a grandfather but someone who could help my grandson take his first step.

Me, I got lucky. From the time I was Nic's age, I was surrounded by people who lent their time and support to help me become someone who participates in life rather than watching from the sidelines. I had a job I loved—a reporter and columnist for the *Edmonton Journal* for thirty-three years—which allowed me to support something I loved so much more: a wife and a family.

And now, a grandson. Yes, I was in a wheelchair. Yes, my means of propelling it was to roll it backwards by pushing on the floor and guiding it by looking back over my shoulder. But I had a grandson. And he was depending on me to help him do this wonderful thing! You think I didn't mist up?

Every detail of that first attempt is engraved in my memory: Sitting in my wheelchair and extending my left leg to his arms. Watching as he slowly climbs up my leg and pulls himself to a standing position, clutching my pants for balance and, I suppose, a sense of security. Reaching down to put his little hands on my knees and, ever so slowly, beginning to wheel backwards, serving as a walker for Nicholas as he pushed me and took his first hesitant steps on this great new adventure.

He got better at it with each passing day. A few weeks later, he was walking on his own. I watched it happen and knew I'd played a part in it. Wheelchair be damned. I was rich beyond measure.

1

"Your Baby is Not Breathing"

My mother, I am told, had a normal pregnancy with very few issues until I actually arrived. Then things went sideways. First, I came out backwards—breech birth, they called it. And I wasn't breathing. Oops.

Remember, now, this was 1958—December 10, to be exact. Modern-day medical technology might have made all the difference. All the doctor could do on that cold day in Grande Prairie, Alberta, was put me in an incubator to keep me warm. Not breathing, but nice and warm. And the longer I went without air, the more my very survival was in the balance.

It was eighteen minutes before I took my first breath. But the relief was short-lived. A minute later, I stopped breathing again, this time for an even longer stretch. But I guess even then I was a stubborn little cuss. Finally, when I was 45 minutes old, I took a breath. And then another one, and another after that. I have no memory of the process, of course, but I must have figured this breathing thing was pretty cool, because I haven't stopped doing it since.

Into the world I came, unable to bend my right arm or open the hand, needing the blanket behind me for support to sit up because I had no balance. But was I excited!

But then the other shoe dropped.

My folks noticed that I wasn't progressing like other babies and had trouble holding my head up. When I was eleven months old, they took me to a specialist, who gave them the word: I had cerebral palsy and, because of that lack of oxygen at birth, the motor area of my brain was damaged. Because the brain was still mainly unexplored territory—"jungle country," some doctors called it—the specifics of the damage were in the lap of the gods. But they would be extensive.

I have long since made my peace with who I am and with my physical limitations. I have studied the enemy. Cerebral palsy is not a disease or a sickness; it is a condition. In fact, I have come to view it as a characteristic of mine: I have cerebral palsy much like I have blue eyes and have—or should I say had?—brown hair. It is, simply, a part of who I am. When I speak to groups about my situation, I can even joke about it. "Think of CP as Canada Post," I tell them. "My brain sends out signals, and God knows where they wind up."

But in 1958, when disabilities were not as widely accepted as they are today, having cerebral palsy leant itself to little if any potential. I spent the majority of my time on the floor, sitting like a frog. I could not swallow—my chin was always covered with saliva. I made noises, but nobody could understand what I was saying. My eyes were crossed and my hands were clenched like a heavyweight fighter's fists. What sort of future, if any, was there for a baby like that?

On the surface, a reasonable question. What no one knew, least of all me, was that those two clenched hands held two aces, superheroes without costumes or capes. To many, they were Harold and Thelma. Six people called them Grandma and Grandpa, but I think I had the greatest honour of all—to me, they were Mom and Dad.

In a sense, my birth problems were a family rerun. My dad came into the world in 1921 with gangrene, a condition in which reduced blood supply kills some cells before they can develop, and thus destroys a considerable mass of body tissue. In Dad's case, the doctors told his parents, it wasn't mere life-threatening. Their son would likely die right there in that North Battleford, Saskatchewan, hospital.

"No," Grandma Tait told them. "If he's going to die, he's going to die at home."

So she and my grandfather took my dad home to their farm, just southwest of Meota, Saskatchewan—with a view of Jackfish Lake—about thirty kilometres north of North Battleford. I guess Dad inherited Grandma's stubbornness gene. For all the dire predictions, he persevered as the youngest of four children and had only a stubbed baby toe on his left foot to show that there'd ever been a problem.

He had an off-the-wall sense of humour, my dad.

My guides, my rocks, my inspiration – there for my wedding as they'd always been there for me: Mom and Dad.

Maybe there is something to this inheritance thing, because people have said the same thing about me. I still laugh at the memories of his greatest antics, like the night he invited some guys to the farm for coffee, spiked it with ex-lax and chortled over the washroom line-ups before hiding in the barn's hay loft when the victims came looking for him, waving pitchforks.

Or the time he climbed into his best friend's car minutes before his buddy picked up his first date ever, and hid on the floorboards behind the front seat for the entire date without making a sound? Or the one that backfired, when he dressed up as a woman for a country dance, then had to run like hell when a young man put the moves on him?

And maybe the best of all, when he proposed to my mom by telling her he didn't think they should get married.

She was crushed. They'd talked about it. They'd been dating. Obviously, the connection was real and meaningful. Their friends considered them an item. And yet there he was, stopping the car on one of their evening drives and saying he didn't think they should get married??? Mom was devastated—until, with his most sinister laugh, he reached over, opened the glove compartment, pulled out a ring box and asked her to marry him. It's a wonder she didn't smack him. They were married December 27, 1955, on my grandfather Murray's farm near Grimshaw, Alberta, Mom's hometown. In keeping with the strong Scottish background they shared, the minister officiating the service wore a kilt. There is no record that Dad flipped it to see if he was wearing anything under it—but I wouldn't have put it past him.

Given his outgoing personality, you might think that Dad would choose a wife with a similar quirkiness. Well, think again. Mom also grew up on a farm, in the Peace River country. She loved being around kids. As a young woman, she also loved playing the piano and going to the Anglican Church with her folks and her two sisters and brother. She obviously didn't have my father's comedic flair, but she was the kindest person I will ever know. Within minutes of meeting someone, she made them feel as if they were the most important person in the world, because for Mom, at that particular moment, they were.

What's that saying—life is what happens while you're planning it? Before they met, both my parents were in Edmonton, planning to attend the University of Alberta. Dad could have taken over the family farm in Saskatchewan from Grandfather Tait, but he said farming wasn't for him—he wanted to become a teacher. The fates had other ideas. He was in Edmonton, getting ready for university, when he contracted polio, which turned out to be mild, as he escaped with restricted movement in his left arm. His roommate in the Edmonton hospital was a tax assessor for the Department of Municipal Affairs and asked Dad to come work for him as a property assessor. Never one to back down from a challenge, with his education plans clearly on at least temporary hold, Dad started working for the provincial government in 1953.

Mom and Dad both wound up working in Grande Prairie, Mom as an elementary school teacher and Dad "knocking on doors, telling people how much they owed the government." They met at a Friday night card party arranged by one of Mom's best friends. I guess you could say they both played their cards right. It was opening night of a lifetime love affair.

2
. . .

Pushing the Pause Button

Card-playing didn't just bring my folks together, it provided one of the unspoken rules upon which they based their lives: you don't waste time moaning about bad cards or rotten luck; you play the hand you're dealt.

Their newborn child had cerebral palsy, a situation that's been known to cause hesitation about adding to the family lest there be a reoccurrence. But my folks had planned on having more than one child. Why would my situation change that? When I was two and a half years old, I got a blonde baby sister, Joan Maureen. Two years later we were presented with a little brother, Bradley Brent. All the while, my parents were working to create the best possible environment for the ongoing battle with CP.

There weren't many services or support systems for kids with cerebral palsy in Grande Prairie. My parents checked around and located a CP clinic in Edmonton. An accommodating boss arranged a transfer for Dad, and in the fall of 1962 we moved to the west end of Edmonton, where I was taken to the clinic a couple of days a week. My memory doesn't provide a lot of details, but I do remember my legs being put in braces in an attempt to straighten them.

Today, I find that a little curious. I mean, I didn't have the balance to stand even if I could, legs straight or crooked. I guess they were exploring all the possibilities, but I gather that, despite their best efforts, not much was happening. Fortunately, Mom and Dad weren't the only stubborn ones in the family.

My uncle Jim on Mom's side was studying at the University of Princeton. His wife, my aunt Evelyn, had read a magazine story about a new treatment technique for brain-injured children at a clinic in Philadelphia that was said to be achieving some amazing results. In August 1963, Uncle Jim called my father, collect, and told him about the program. In no uncertain terms, Uncle Jim said he wasn't ending the call until Dad agreed to bring me to Philadelphia.

They fought and argued, as they always did. But, since long-distance plans of calling anywhere for $9.95 a month were decades away, Dad thought of the ever-growing telephone bill, and gave in.

"Good," said Uncle Jim. "The program is called The Institutes for the Achievement of Human Potential. Look it up."

The Institutes, nestled in the quaint town of Chestnut Hill just north of Philadelphia, was started in 1955 by Glenn Doman. Doman received his degree in physical therapy from the University of Pennsylvania in 1940, and, after serving with distinction in the Second World War for the US, he began studies that led to pioneering a new therapy for brain-injured kids. Doman and his staff decided not to treat the symptoms of brain injury—the spastic legs, or the clenched fist or the slurred speech—but to stimulate the brain to get going again.

Because of the lack of oxygen at birth, my brain was on pause. The rest of my body was growing, but the signals from my brain were just not getting to it. Doman had proven, early on, that by training the undamaged brain cells to take over from the damaged ones, there was vast improvement. The Institutes had provided treatment for kids with conditions such as cerebral palsy, epilepsy, autism, Down syndrome, dyslexia, attention deficit disorders and many more. Yet, when my parents were looking for support to go to The Institutes, there was basically none. In fact, word of what The Institutes was doing wasn't very widespread in Canada.

More alarming, though, was the Canadian medical profession's lack of support for the idea of what Doman was doing. The program, critics said, was not medically proven. Dad went to visit our family doctor, a true Irishman named O'Rooney with a big heart, who was always very good to me. But when Dad asked him about the possibility of taking me to Philadelphia, his answer was clear and definite: we'd be wasting our time and money, because there were many other programs in Canada and Alberta that could help us just as much.

Dad's Scottish stubbornness gene kicked in. He thanked the good doctor for his advice, and started making plans for Philadelphia. It couldn't have been easy. There were many things to be worked out, especially the financing, not just for the travel but for The Institutes' fee. I asked him so many times how much those fees were. His standing answer: "It was all worth it and more."

In the spring of 1964, he and Mom got it together and the three of us took our first trip to Philadelphia, and the first steps of an incredible journey that would change my life.

The Institutes' system was based on the premise that brain-injured kids would have the biggest opportunity to improve if they had the treatment given to them by the two people who were the closest to them—their parents—and that the family home was a much more caring place for exercises than in an institutional setting. After five eighteen-hour days of extensive training and reams and reams of papers to study and sign, Mom and Dad brought me home to put the program in place. I still shake my head in wonderment at how they managed it, and the mental and physical price they must have paid.

The most important step of the exercises was called a cross-pattern, designed to teach me to crawl. I'd never learned how as a baby, certainly couldn't do it now with my stiffer-than-boards limbs, and with my brain on pause, it couldn't send out the signals to get me started. So, put yourself in my parents' shoes for a moment and consider what they were facing. Do the exercise with them—and remember that you've got a two-year-old daughter and a son not yet turned one, with all the hectic time and care that implies—and that the five-year-old you will be flexing and cajoling and coaxing through the discomfort on a daily basis is your own son or daughter.

You lift me onto the kitchen table, on my stomach with my head on its left side, my left elbow bent, my hand on the table, my left knee bent just like it would be if I was crawling flat on my stomach.

Now, time to get me moving, which, by the way, you can't do by yourself. Every cross-pattern requires three people: one person to turn my head, one on my left side and another on my right. When the person holding my head begins turning it, the people moving my arms and legs follow suit. Every pattern goes on for five minutes. Oh, and stay cheerful and positive no matter how much you might want to cry. Got to give off those positive vibes.

How're you holding up?

Now consider that, as my parents began to figure out how best to put some sort of plan into operation even on a short-term basis, they had to factor in the other joker in the deck—The Institutes' instruction that, because I was five and there was a lot of work to do, the patterning should be repeated eight times a day, every day, at the same times within one-hour intervals, so my brain could grow accustomed to a schedule and start to look for the newest installment.

Couldn't be done. Not without a miracle. In their heart of hearts, my parents must have known that. But a wonderful thing happened. They didn't get their miracle. They got dozens of them.

• • •

Allan Kissack, my dad's best friend back in Meota, had moved to Edmonton and now lived six blocks south of us in the Lynnwood suburb. Word had gotten around on our return from The Institutes about what my parents faced. When Dad explained to Allan the patterning process and what it would involve, he and his wife, Dorothy, made an incredible offer. They wouldn't just learn to assist with the patterning, they would find other volunteers and teach them to do it.

Edie Dehid, a neighbour four houses west, took it upon herself to spread the word that the Taits needed help. The response was so overwhelming that Edie devised a schedule, assigning specific volunteers to specific times, with all the juggling that implies. Almost overnight she had forty neighbours ready to help.

The schedule was almost military in its approach. Patterns were scheduled at nine, ten and eleven in the morning, and resumed after lunch break at one, two and four in the afternoon, then seven and eight in the evening. Years later, Mom recalled that first day as organized chaos.

The Kissack family spent most of the day with us, helping however they could. Aunt Dorothy and Uncle Bill Beattie drove to Edmonton from Grande Prairie for the weekend and provided great support. After the first day of patterning, my parents were exhausted. Yet, they had little time to rest. The doorbell would start ringing again just before 9:00 a.m. as another three volunteers would show up for the day's first pattern.

Yes, the patterning hurt in the beginning. I remember that. My limbs had never been used before, so some discomfort was natural. The key was not to stop the pattern until the end of the five minutes so the brain could get as much uninterrupted stimulation as possible. I wore a t-shirt and a pair of shorts. To make my legs slide easier on the kitchen table, Mom would rub them with cornstarch before we started.

Word of the incredible thing happening at the Tait house was working its way through the community. Within three months of starting, the original number of volunteers doubled to eighty, and they all were encouraged by the news from of our third trip to Philadelphia for an evaluation in the fall of 1964. In just six months of patterning, I was assessed as having the neuromuscular level of a four-year-old, an improve-

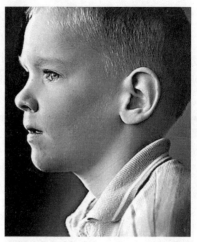

Five years old and ready to go to work on a job that would last five years and involve about one hundred people: the battle to make my body do what it was told.

ment of nearly two years from my first diagnosis.

Success was measured in the joy of small gains. Mom said one of the first signs of improvement she saw was that I could swallow by myself. I remember gaining a new sense of balance, assisting me in something as simple as sitting up. The key was the ever-increasing support. By Christmas, we had 116 people coming to our home for ten minutes once a day to help. Many of that number stayed with us for the entire time we did the program. They took pride in the gains as though they were family, which in a real sense they were. I remember, many times, a volunteer would see me do something and say, "You couldn't do that last week."

It was years later before I truly understood the magnitude of the undertaking and the dedication of the people who gave up chunks of their time to turn the near-impossible to reality. Because that was the thing—it couldn't be just a casual commit-ment. The key was doing patterns hour after hour, day after day, week after week. When The Institutes stressed to my folks that they had to be done every day, they weren't kidding. Birthdays? Christmas? Easter? Do the patterns. Cam was sick? Too bad. Do the patterns. Mom and Dad even took a patterning table with us on summer holidays so we wouldn't miss a session.

(There was one time a pattern was interrupted. Dad got home from work just after 5:00 p.m. and took over the evening patterns so Mom could attend to Joan and Brad. It was a Wednesday night. There was a bench-clearing brawl on *Hockey Night in Canada*. Dad stopped the pattern so I could watch the fight. Don Cherry would have been proud.)

The reasoning was sound. Research had shown that if a few patterns were missed, the brain would erase some of the progress it had made, and take even longer to reinstate itself—which, of course, was fuel for the fire for the medical community to cry that such an intensive program resulted in marriage breakdowns. Mom was having none of it. In an interview, she said she thought that our situation actually brought our family closer.

But the commitment—by neighbours, friends, relatives, people my folks didn't even know until they turned up at the door to volunteer—was beyond belief. Many came once a week at specific times. In the morning and mid-afternoons, the majority were housewives who came to do a pattern after they got their kids off to school. Those from the neighbourhood walked— sometimes together—to our home. Others drove from other communities in the west end.

Edie Dehid kept track of the schedule. When volunteers had to miss a pattern, they would call her and she would arrange with someone from her list to fill the position. On the weekends, natu- rally, there were fewer people available. No problem. Those who could make it stayed for two patterns. Sometimes we would begin the pattern short a person, but like clockwork, the missing person would burst through the door and join the group. After lunch, more housewives came in for the afternoon patterns, many with curlers in their hair. While they did patterns they watched their favourite soap opera. (Naturally, I saw them, too. Almost fifty years later, I really can't see a lot has progressed in the storyline.) The Bank of Montreal, where Mom and Dad did their banking, was in a strip mall across the street from our home. Soon after we began the program, three staff members walked across the street every Tuesday and Thursday to help with the one o'clock pattern.

In the five years the pattern program was in place, the volunteers' physical contributions—turning my head and moving my arms and legs—were invaluable. But their emotional support was perhaps an even greater gift. Five or ten minutes before a pattern began, I'd be looking forward to their arrival. People would knock, ring the doorbell or just walk in. We'd chat for a few brief moments, and when the clock struck the top of the hour, Mom lifted me onto the table and the patterns began. I didn't realize until I was an adult the benefits I was getting from interacting with so many people at such a young age. It helped me tremendously with my social skills as I got older.

It's difficult, if not impossible, to single out volunteers. They all mean the world to me. But there are a few who made an unforgettable impression. With apologies to every one of the others, who hold permanent places in my mind and heart, I'll mention one or two, starting with the wonderful Mrs. B.

Early in the patterning program, the doorbell rang one evening. It was Mrs. B—Maxine Bradley—her husband Bill, son Barth and daughter Judy. They came over after hearing of the program and wanted to help. It was the start of a lifetime friendship.

For the Bradleys, doing the patterns wasn't enough. So, Mom taught Mrs. B how to do the hand exercises that the folks in Philadelphia had suggested. Every Friday morning after taking part in the nine o'clock pattern, Mrs. B would put me through my paces as we sat at the kitchen table. One exercise involved two green plastic glasses and two coins, the objective being to pour the coins from one glass to another, ten times in a row without letting the glasses touch while pouring. If they did, I had to start all over again. Years later, I am still looking for my first bartending job.

Another exercise was teaching me how to screw the top on a bottle of dish soap. To develop my sense of touch, I had to identify heads and tails on a coin while blindfolded. Mrs. B was the soul of patience, her infectious laughter filling the house. I credit her with developing coordination in my hands; she is, without question, the reason I am able to type. But hand work on Fridays was only part of our friendship. Our families began sharing Christmas Eve together, a tradition that lasted four decades.

Many of the details of those days I learned years later in conversations with my parents and people like Mrs. B. Some of them were amazing. For instance, I had no idea that my mother— my quiet, soft-spoken mother, who loved to play piano and preferred being in the background rather than as the centre of attention—was made of pure steel.

There must have been private times when the daily load grew almost too heavy to bear, when the alarm went off and all she wanted to do was curl up, pull the blankets over her head and let the world go to hell. If there were, I never saw them. Dad would go off to work at 7:30 a.m., and there would be Mom, doing what must be done and more, the glue that held the family together and kept the fear outside.

Mom did all my personal care, toileting, dressing and feeding me, on top of running the household and raising Joan and Brad. She also was in charge of my discipline, and my physical problems earned me no Get Out of Jail Free card. When I was out of line, I got the wooden spoon treatment on my bottom just as Joan and Brad did. In fact, when I was really out of line, she told me she was going to ship me off to Red Deer to Michener Centre, a residence for kids with mental and physical disabilities. I apologized, begging for forgiveness and not to be sent away. Luckily for me, she never did.

Her energy level must have been phenomenal. Every weekday started with her giving me a salt bath followed by a very brisk rubdown to improve my blood circulation. Then came breakfast, as monitored by The Institutes, which also ruled that sweets were out, because it had been proven that sugar played havoc with the growth of the brain. Chocolate, ice cream, cake—all the good things kids love to eat—were off limits and not allowed in the house, which probably was unfair to Brad and Joan.

As we were finishing, the front door would open again and again as the volunteers arrived for the patterning. Mom was more than just a part of that process. In the initial stages, three volunteers were needed to do a pattern. But as I grew, The Institutes suggested someone keep their hands on my feet to provide more control, and it was my mother who answered the call, taking part in every pattern.

Did I mention the home schooling? When I turned six and had so much more mobility, Mom thought it was time to start teaching me Grade 1. She didn't know how long the patterning program would continue, but since it was working, she decided the best thing was to keep me at home and keep doing it.

The Edmonton Public School Board suggested the Homebound Program, where a teacher would come to our home every weekday for one hour, the time broken down into spelling, math, language, science and other subjects. I couldn't write or print, so in Grade 2 Mom and Dad got me an electric typewriter from the Cerebral Palsy Association—and that's when I started typing, first with my right hand, and then my left. Slowly, with much practice, I reached the point where I could use both hands, and I have Mrs. B to thank for limbering up my hands and fingers.

That's how I took the first four grades of my schooling, in the afternoons from three to four, adjusting the patterning schedule a little to make room for my teacher's daily visit. One of our friends brought a school desk to the house so that I could sit in it during class, which was pretty cool. Helen Westbrook was my Grade 1 and 2 teacher; Mr. Whitney taught me in Grade 3; and Miss Derksen came to our house for Grade 4. And, lucky for me, I passed all four grades. I thank them all, but mostly I thank my mom, who somehow found the time to make it happen.

Sometimes, well-meaning volunteers would bring their children. It was a nice thought, but I didn't have time to play. When they arrived at nine in the morning, my day was already three hours old.

Again by The Institutes' decree, as soon as I was done a pattern, I had to crawl on my own steam for ten minutes, which required some ingenuity on the part of my parents. The first tries were on the living room carpet, but I stopped often, which defeated the purpose. During one of our trips to Philadelphia, they suggested a crawling box of eight feet, with carpet on the bottom and each side. Better—but I raised my head whenever I turned from side to side, and we'd been told that my brain would get a better workout if my head was kept as low as possible. So a neighbour designed a rope system that went across the top of the box.

But, damn, that was hard to do. I was taught how to curl my toes and dig into the carpet to move myself forward. My arms—clearly not as strong as my legs—helped me pull forward. There were times when I was just so tired, and frustrated, I would stop in the middle of the crawling box and stay there. But Mom had a trick up her sleeve. Because we were travelling to Philadelphia so often, I had fallen in love with airplanes. Whenever I stopped crawling, she would put my favourite model aircraft at the end of the crawling box to help me keep going.

By that time, doing the patterns didn't hurt at all; in fact, once my muscles had become limbered up, they felt good. The crawling was the hardest part of the whole program, and I crawled on the rug for two hours throughout the day. No wheelchair for me in the house. The Institutes said it was best to let me crawl or creep from room to room, which would help my brain grow even more. Mom sewed pieces of leather on my pants to protect my knees. All I needed was a cowboy hat, and I was ready to help the Lone Ranger chase the Cavendish gang.

The crawling didn't end it. Other exercise programs were waiting, one involving a plastic mask that went over my mouth and nose for one minute every hour, a very small tube at the end of the mask allowing a minimal amount of oxygen. Objective: making me out of breath increased the development of my lungs and served as a cardio workout.

Oh, yeah, I also had that eye problem. For the first five years of my life, they stared at each other. We were taught an exercise using a pen flashlight, where my mother would slowly move it to the middle of my nose. This forced my eyes to converge on it, and then they would follow it back to where Mom started it.

There were other stumbling blocks to our daily existence. For one, there was the matter of the music.

Mom enjoyed her piano playing, and she gave lessons to neighbourhood kids. Dad was a great clarinet player in his day, although he couldn't read a note of music. But the folks at The Institutes said if I heard any music, it would be a distraction and perhaps even undo some of the results from the patterning. So, music was put on hold. Whenever we were watching television and there was music, someone would jump up and turn the volume down. Then, when we saw someone talking, we turned it up again. Simple, right?

There were so many things going on in our home, yet Mom made sure the important occasions—Christmas, Easter, birthdays—all had her special touch. Then, in 1967, she gave us all a scare. She was washing the back of her left ear and found a brown mark that wouldn't come off. She went to our doctor, who referred Mom to a specialist—and the news wasn't good. She had melanoma, a type of skin cancer.

Dad was working in Yellowknife, on loan from the Alberta government. I was on my hands and knees in the hallway when Mom called Dad and gave him the news. It was the first time I had seen my mother cry.

"Harold, I'm sick. Can you come home?"

Dad was on the next plane to Edmonton because Mom's condition was very serious. I wasn't told until I was an adult that the doctors said they could operate, take half of Mom's ear off, but gave her only eight months to live.

In an act of what I think was pure heroism, we never missed a pattern. Mom arranged for help to come in and look after us three kids while she was in the hospital undergoing surgery. Even when she got home and was recuperating in her bed down the hall, she still was in command. "I think I heard you say something, but really, that isn't the best idea how to do that," she would say, before calmly explaining how it should be done.

Mom had always been quite religious and was a faithful churchgoer. After her cancer diagnosis, she asked Jesus Christ to come into her life as her personal saviour and credited Him for her miraculous survival. When she told me about her battle, she also said having so many people coming into the house to help with patterns was a great source of support for her.

Mom died in 2008, thirteen months after Dad. I treasure the memories. Whatever I've done, whatever I may yet accomplish, I owe it all to them. And if, as some have said, I have a compassionate side to me, it's another gift from my mother.

3
· · ·

Is This Really a Story?

My parents never asked for publicity for what they were doing with me. Rather, they shied away from it, especially Mom. But word was getting out that something pretty incredible was happening on Eighty-seventh Avenue in Edmonton.

The Bank of Montreal sent a writer to Edmonton to do a story for their national employee magazine, since several of their staff members from the Lynnwood branch were helping us with patterns. It ran in the Christmas issue in 1964, complete with a photo spread. From there, it just grew.

John Klemm was a neighbour who worked as a ticket agent for Air Canada and was a freelance writer. He also did patterns and wrote a piece for Chatelaine magazine. Another volunteer mentioned it to someone at CBC television, and suddenly there was producer Jack Emack in our living room, pitching Mom and Dad about a 30-minute nationally televised documentary. They balked at first, but he sold them with the thought of the hope such a show might bring to other parents of brain-injured kids.

Jack and a television crew literally moved into our home for a week. There were cameras, cables and spotlights everywhere. Jack and the crew were with us from six in the morning until I went to bed.

Some of our volunteers were reluctant to go on camera. Others thought it was pretty cool. A few even asked if they could go home and quickly take their curlers out and then come back. Jack understood their concerns, but asked that they please stay, because he wanted to capture the grassroots of the program.

I really enjoyed having CBC around. Maybe that early taste of media's semi-controlled chaos whet my appetite for my future career. I became friends with many of the crew and we shared quite a few laughs.

During their last evening with us, Jack had a sit-down interview with Mom and Dad about what we were doing. Between a cough and what I'm sure must have been a case of on-camera nerves, Mom required countless glasses of water before she could get enough voice back to answer questions. Dad, on the other hand, was having a hell of a good time, dressed smartly in his crisp white shirt and dark tie. It was the 1960s and everyone was smoking on television—even Dad in the interview.

Jack's last question still gives me the chills. What did Dad hope to have me doing in the following two years? "I hope to have him walking," Dad said before he took a drag on his cigarette. "Or maybe developing these three steps of him walking, and I can take him by the hand, and we can walk along together."

Out of the hours of film came a 28-minute show called *100 For Cameron*—the 100 representing all the volunteers who were helping us. It went across the regional network October 22, 1966, and was so very well received the decision was made to run it nationally. We heard from many relatives across Canada saying several of their friends who saw the show cried through the entire half hour—not, we hoped, about the fact that I was disabled and could now do a few things, but as a response to how so many people were coming together to help us.

• • •

I was gaining mobility all the time. I could even walk for a period on my own, and whenever he could, Dad had me walk to show people how much I had improved. We were at a hockey game in Kelowna in the summer of 1968 with players from the National Hockey League, including Frank Mahovlich. We attended a dinner after the game, where Dad quickly got me out of my chair and I took about fifteen steps before I fell backwards into his arms. Mahovlich must have been impressed. The next Christmas, we got a card from him and his wife, Marie.

If we had company over for dinner, Dad would have me walk for them. Maybe it was Dad's way of showing people how far we had come in the patterning. Or perhaps he was trying to get me to walk increasingly so that eventually I would be able to master it. Because that was what I was constantly told, that if I was going to do anything productive and meaningful with my life, I had to walk. That was the be-all and end-all. Part of that was the era—the mid-1960s, when people with disabilities in wheelchairs were not accepted fully into society.

My grandparents on Mom's side, Joseph and Eva Murray, sold the family farm and bought the house next door to ours. It wasn't until I was an adult that I appreciated that their move to Edmonton was a wonderful show of support for Mom and Dad. Still, the push for me to walk was on. One Sunday after I washed my hands before dinner, Grandpa Murray shook his head and looked at me before saying, "It's a bloody shame that boy can't walk."

But, on the other hand, we had come so far. I felt a great sense of new independence from being able to stand, to swallow, to open my hands and to start forming words, which led to me being able to talk.

As 1968 rolled out, changes were coming in the program.

We heard that someone in the Philadelphia area had designed a machine to do patterns, and we had one shipped to Edmonton. Mom put me in the machine and strapped my arms and legs into padded grooves and my head into a helmet-like apparatus. I felt like I was in training for the Apollo 11 moon mission.

With a series of pulleys, Mom operated the machine by pulling two big levers together, but it put brutal strain on her shoulders. Once again a volunteer helped us out, a mechanic named Bill Bachon, who built a motor to run the patterning machine. In fact, that was the first time I had my name in the *Edmonton Journal*—a reporter came out to write a story about Bachon's invention.

The folks at The Institutes also suggested that I had reached a plateau of improvement. And really, I had, considering I was standing on my own and walking on my own. Dad counted how many steps I could take on my own before falling and the most was thirty-six. Sure, it was dangerous, but the mobility I had was priceless. Even though the goal was for me to walk, the very fact that I could sit upright and use a wheelchair was a major victory.

We decided to cut down to four patterns a day from eight, which was really good for Mom. Since we had a motor on the patterning machine, it meant there were fewer and fewer people coming and going and I really missed that. The volunteers provided me with such encouragement and shared their spirit of hope. We had more than twenty-five people coming into our home every day and when they stopped, I really felt a sense of loss.

The Institutes had a new exercise for us to do to try to help me in the quest to walk. We raised a metal ladder horizontally over a rubber mat and I used my arms to reach as far as I could, rung by rung, then moved my legs and feet forward until I was upright. And then I started over. And over, and over...

One of my biggest problems was adjusting my sense of balance, particularly when I was attempting to walk on my own. There was strength in my arms and legs, but I had a tendency to fall backwards, which was my biggest fear. I had a few bad falls when I started walking with the ladder, but over time I became more confident and the falls weren't so frequent. Over a few months I began to get better at it. I had callouses on my hands from hand-walking hanging from the rungs for about an hour and a half each day. I find it rather amazing that that was basically the only injury I encountered from the program. The patterns did not hurt at all; in fact, moving my arms, legs and neck felt good. The only time it was hard was when I was sick with a cold or the flu.

I was growing, too. As a 10-year-old boy, doing patterns was getting to be harder because of my height and weight. So, in the fall of 1969, we made our final trip to The Institutes. It was time to carry on with my new life with my new mobility—without the program.

● ● ●

My parents gave up so much—but perhaps Joan and Brad gave up even more.

Most of the attention was on me as a child, not only because I had cerebral palsy but because of the intense program we undertook. Mom and Dad shared so much time with me and I know Joan and Brad were short-changed. Although they never have openly told me, I know they somewhat resent missing out on many things. I feel horrible about this. But, having said that, I have no doubt in my mind Mom and Dad would have done the same for them in a second.

In our adult years we became very distant. I know I was part of the problem, and maybe I expected too much, but I really miss having had a brother to go on trips with and share family gatherings with my sister and her family. I understand and respect why that isn't the case, but the sense of loss will always be there.

4
····

My Personal Tour Guide

In all, we made eighteen trips from Edmonton to Philadelphia over five years. The Institutes' staff would evaluate my progress and make suggestions for the next couple of months. Mom, Dad and I made the first two trips together, but after factoring in Mom's aversion to travel and to leaving Joan and Brad with someone, not to mention the additional expense, from then on it was just Dad and me.

On our first trip together, I promised myself I wouldn't cry. Mom always bought me a new toy to play with on the plane and she said I could sleep with her the night before we left. No tears, I assured her. There weren't any at the airport when we said goodbye, and no tears, either, when we went into the Toronto airport and walked by the coffee shop where the three of us had eaten during those first two trips. But after the meal was served on the flight from Toronto to New York, when the sky outside was pitch black, when I started playing with the blue farm tractor Mom had given me that morning, the floodgates opened.

At 25,000 feet in the air, 4,000 miles from home, I missed my mom. After that big cry, Dad and I formed an even tighter bond than we already had—not at local baseball diamonds or hockey rinks, but in airports, hotels, cabs and, of course, at The Institutes. We would leave on Saturday morning, fly into Toronto, take the connecting flight to New York, and then the short hop to Philadelphia. I used a wheelchair in airports and hotels, and Dad took his 8-mm movie camera to film my progress. We had some wonderful trips, and amazing things kept happening.

One of the volunteers doing patterns worked for Imperial Oil, a major sponsor of *Hockey Night in Canada*. Not only did he arrange to get two tickets to see my favourite team, the Maple Leafs, play the Rangers, he contacted someone with the Leafs to arrange a meeting with my hockey hero, Toronto goaltender Johnny Bower. Dad took me down to the dressing room and we seemed to wait forever. Bower was the last one out of the shower and greeted us wearing only a towel.

A few years later, we got to see another game between the Leafs and the Detroit Red Wings. Gordie Howe and Eddie Shack were matched against each other all night long, which was a real treat to watch.

In 1967, we made a side trip to Ottawa, staying with Harold Hayes, a friend of Dad's from his days back in Meota, and got to watch the Hamilton Tiger-Cats play the Saskatchewan

Boy, am I glad Gordie Howe was kidding! Mr. Hockey uses me as target to show my son, Darren, the elbow that levelled opponents.

Roughriders in the Grey Cup game. We were disappointed when the Ticats lost 24–1, but were amazed by the generosity of some slightly drunk Hamilton fans. As we waited for a cab after the game, they saw me in the chair and kept filling my jacket pockets with money. It came to $45. And the surprises weren't over.

On the flight to Montreal the next morning, as we started to work our way home—pre-boarded as usual—Dad nudged me as passengers began to file down the aisle. "I think that's John Diefenbaker and his wife," he said softly of the former prime minister of Canada. It so happened they were seated right behind us. When Mr. Diefenbaker started discussing the British North American Act, Dad smiled. "It's him, alright," he said.

When we landed in Ottawa, Diefenbaker and his wife were the last off the aircraft. He saw Dad putting on my jacket as we waited for the plane to clear. The former prime minister stopped to say hello, asked where we were headed, turned to leave, then turned back.

"Son," he asked in that voice that thundered through the House of Commons, "do you like dogs?"

I said I did.

"When you get home, you send me a letter in Ottawa and I will send you a picture of my dog and me," he said.

As soon as we got home from that trip, I typed a letter to Diefenbaker. A few weeks later, a brown envelope came from the House of Commons with a letter and, sure enough, a picture of his dog and himself.

That same year, Dad got a phone call from another childhood friend, Keith Allen, who'd played defence on the Meota hockey team for which Dad played goal, moved on to a brief NHL career and on up the chain of command to become the first coach of the expansion team, the Philadelphia Flyers. Keith had heard of the trips to The Institutes and had a message for Dad: "From now on, you stay with us when you're here," he said.

He did better than that. We stayed with the Allen family—Mrs. Allen, sons Brad and Blake and daughter Tracy—in their home in Bryn Mawr, Pennsylvania, just west of Philadelphia. They picked us up at the airport and drove us to and from The Institutes. When we arrived in Philadelphia one Sunday afternoon, we were greeted by the entire Allen family, and informed that supper that night would be a hot dog and a pop at the Spectrum, where the Flyers would be playing the St. Louis Blues.

We went straight from the airport to the rink, where Keith gave Dad and me a great behind-the-scenes tour of what went on before a hockey game. He then took me by myself and wheeled me to the centre of the Flyers' dressing room. Keith wanted to see which one of his players would be the first to come and shake my hand. It was Flyers captain Lou Angotti, followed by the rest of the team, including future Hall of Fame goaltender Bernie Parent.

And just when we thought the night couldn't get any better, it did. When we were walking to Keith's car in the parking lot after the game, legendary goaltender Glenn Hall, who was waiting for the St. Louis team bus, stopped Keith to chat. Dad and I were then introduced to him.

● ● ●

My dad showed me many things during our times in Philadelphia—about life, and about himself.

One noon hour as we sat at the Philadelphia train station, we watched workers making improvements on the track: four Caucasians, one African-American. When lunchtime came, the white workers sat together on one side of the track, and the African-American sat by himself on the other.

"C'mon," Dad said, tipping my chair to go over the tracks. "We're going to visit that gentleman." And we did just that, garnering dirty looks from other watchers. Dad didn't care.

He was from Canada and he would talk to anyone and be their friend—one of the greatest lessons he taught me.

Dad and I would spend all day Monday at The Institutes and visit Dr. Eugene Spitz on Tuesday. Dr. Spitz was a noted brain surgeon, and although he never operated on me, he provided great encouragement and council. On the Wednesday we would fly home, and I will never forget one trip. We caught the train from Philadelphia to New York and took a cab from Grand Central Station to JFK International Airport. The fare was eight dollars. Even. After the cabbie got our luggage and my wheelchair out, he asked Dad for a tip.

"Fuck off," Dad retorted without missing a beat.

I was eight years old and had never heard this new greeting. Thirty minutes before we landed in Edmonton, I asked Dad what it meant.

"Ask your mother," he said.

So, as soon as we landed, I did. And that may have been our quietest ride home from the Edmonton International Airport.

5

Learning—the Hard Way

And then, suddenly, it was time for me—no pun intended—to take the next step.

To make a life, I would need to function in the world outside my home. To do that, I would require an education both in academics and in the everyday business of life. As usual, my mom had the path figured out in advance.

After a lot of research, she found the Glenrose School Hospital, a school for kids with physical and emotional disabilities that had opened in 1966 and offered physio, occupational and speech therapy, in addition to academic classes. Near the end of Grade 4 of my home-schooling classes, we went there for an assessment interview by assistant principal Henry Unrau, who tested my mental skills. Apparently I passed, because it was decided that I should be enrolled in all three phases.

To this day, that has baffled me. I mean, I had just spent the past five years of my life, fourteen hours a day, doing exercises—and now I had to do some more? Mom and Dad said it was a good idea, so I went along with it—as though I had a choice. And, in

September 1969, I was wheeled onto an Edmonton Handibus and went off to my first-ever day of out-of-home schooling.

My education started early.

Sitting in a wheelchair all day was something new to me, since the Philadelphia program wanted me to be on my hands and knees, creeping around the house as much as possible. An orderly I would come to know and like, Orval Taschuk, had met me at the front door and wheeled me to my classroom. But when it was time to go home I had to make my own way down to the bus, and there was nobody around to push me. I knew going down on my hands and knees wasn't an option—and even if it was, I'd never make my bus.

One of my new classmates, Derrick Coles, had cerebral palsy similar to mine and thus the same problem. And there he was, leaving the classroom on his own by looking back over his shoulder and propelling his chair backwards by pushing on the floor with his feet. Hell, I could do that. (It worked so well that to this day I still wheel myself backwards. My arms are strong, but I have trouble with coordination in wheeling myself forward, so backwards is the easier way to go.) And, just like other kids, I was going to school.

My teacher in Grade 5 was Mrs. Crone, who knew I was the new kid in school and made me feel very comfortable. Classroom sizes were quite small with only eight or nine students. Cerebral palsy, muscular dystrophy, spina bifida and curvature of the spine were among the majority of physical disabilities on Glenrose school's second floor. The third floor was for able-bodied kids who had emotional or psychological issues.

I'd started making friends among my classmates but soon was jolted by one of the sad realities of Glenrose. One of them, Artie, had missed a few weeks of school because he was sick. One morning I raised my hand just after we sang "O Canada" and asked when Artie was coming back to school.

Mrs. Crone paused and cleared her throat. She was clearly uncomfortable.

"I have some really bad news," she said with her voice breaking just a little. "Artie has been very sick. And, last night, he... he passed away."

I'd never had anyone close to me pass away. I didn't know how to think, feel or act. Even though I had not known Artie well and only for a few months, I felt a tremendous loss. How could this be? Artie was 10 years old. It was a rude awakening to an awful truth: there'd be other Arties, at least one almost every year as the afflictions that brought them to Glenrose took their toll. We would see a classmate battling muscular dystrophy slowly fading as muscles weakened. And, one day, a teacher would give us the news that we'd lost another friend.

For me, that first year was strictly Snakes 'n' Ladders, part excitement, part frustration. Take, for instance, the matter of those exercise classes that I didn't want anyway.

Unknown to me, I had one strike coming in. The Glenrose people didn't like The Institutes' program. I'd hear whispers among the instructors: "He's that Tait boy. He was on that damned Philadelphia program." To me, it was an insult to my mom and dad and to all the volunteers who'd helped us.

So I took matters into my own hands. When they wanted me to make a fist, I opened my hands. When they wanted me to straighten my leg, I bent it. When they wanted me to make the "R" sound, I made the "L." The attitude and the fact that I was being taken out of the academic classes to do the therapy, which meant I had tons of homework, triggered a meeting and a decision that I no longer needed the exercises. Score one for that Tait boy.

● ● ●

Time out. I need to explain something.

I've made a point of not allowing any bitterness over my physical state, and I've tried to live my life with that attitude. But in one sense it's a bit of a lie. I am bitter about my education—not for what I was taught, but for what I wasn't. In my view, kids with disabilities weren't pushed hard enough during my school years, and probably aren't today, because the people doing the teaching, however dedicated and well-meaning, saw our disabilities as limits to our potentialities, and therefore didn't see any point in subjecting us to the additional pressures and failures that they felt would be the inevitable result.

There were some wonderful, caring teachers and care staff at Glenrose, and I will be forever grateful to them. There were also some who were thoughtless, some who were just putting in the time and had no thought of helping us push the limits of our potential—and, yes, one or two who were just plain cruel. I suppose anyone could look back on his or her school years and say the same thing, but when you add in the disability factor that made us totally dependent upon them, "school days" take on another dimension.

For instance, Glenrose had nursing staff to help us get our jackets off at school and help with toileting at recess and feeding at lunch. This was my introduction to having paid staff help me with basic personal functions, something that would be with me for the rest of my life.

It took me a while to get comfortable with the idea of having someone other than Mom and Dad helping me go to the bathroom. In fact, I soiled myself several times while sitting in class, because I was ashamed to ask the teacher to call the nursing office for someone to come help me. I don't know why I felt that way but I did. It made for very uncomfortable bus rides home from school, and Mom would always clean me up before supper, but it was humiliating, something I really struggled with.

My parents were sympathetic but realistic, calling it an issue I had to tackle, especially if I wanted to be out in public at school. It took a few months but I wrapped my head around it and called for help when I needed it.

So, we had this essential service, handled for the most part by caring staff who treated us with dignity and respect. But, however strict and well intentioned the screening process, some misfits are going to slip through the cracks. Some of the things that I was exposed to by staff were downright revolting.

One noon hour, I was talking to a friend and he had to have a bowel movement. An orderly took the boy's pants down, lifted him out of his wheelchair, brought him over to me and put his anus in my face for a good ten seconds. The orderly had a good laugh; I almost threw up. Another orderly used to stand right in front me, then turn around and pass gas in my face. We were sworn at and called names, and made fun of by some of the nursing staff.

I wanted to blow the whistle on them, but one of the early lessons for people with disabilities is to face reality. I feared the possible retaliation, which could be much worse. I also knew staff would deny any accusation to their supervisor. For the same reason, I never told my parents. Instead, I bit my tongue and concentrated on the positives: I was in school, and making friends; I had some teachers who really did care; and by seventh grade, I had found my dream.

● ● ●

I'm not sure when the writing dream was born. Maybe it was bubbling in me all along. (Jim Taylor says he knew when he was six years old that he would be a writer someday—not what he'd write, only that he would, and the belief never faded.) So maybe it's an in-the-genes thing, like freckles or left-handedness or an aversion to Brussels sprouts. Whatever it was, I had it—big time.

And—fair is fair—I had teachers who encouraged it and helped make the early successes happen.

Our Grade 6 teacher was Lorne Good, who had mild cerebral palsy. He walked with a slight limp and I always remember he had wonderful patience with us and true empathy for his students. On the other hand, Good was a real taskmaster and demanded we work hard and put in a good effort. He knew what it took to be successful and we all learned from his example.

I got another break when we moved into Grade 7. Our teacher was Ben Flescher, a man who had contracted polio in the 1950s; in fact, he was on the same polio ward as my father. Flescher used a wheelchair and could use one leg to propel himself forward. Like Lorne Good, he taught us a great deal about living with a physical disability. Flescher had a good command of the English language and was a fine writer in his own right. Before he returned to teaching after contracting polio, he wrote a weekly column for the *Edmonton Journal* as a television reviewer. He repeatedly reminded us that writing such a column was something someone with a physical disability could do for a living. That always stuck with me.

Strangely enough, the early writing urge came from radio when I was in seventh grade. CHED was an AM giant playing Top 40 music. But it also featured a former *Journal* reporter named Eddie Keen serving as an editorialist who, by and large, spoke for the little guy in Edmonton. Eddie had two editorials a day, one running at 7:00 a.m. and again at 8:00, the other at noon and 5:30 p.m. Eddie's words caught my ear and I listened to him religiously. Eventually, I got up the nerve to call him when I got home from school and asked him to mail me a copy of an editorial I especially liked. When it came, I studied it, looking at the words Eddie used, the way he constructed his sentences and thoughts.

Eddie became my hero, to the point where I decided I could start writing my own editorials after I did my homework in the evening. I wrote two a day—just like Eddie. Each editorial was a page of copy, double-spaced. I wrote in all capital letters and used three dots in between periods—just like Eddie. (I later found out the three dots is a common practice in broadcast copy, telling announcers where to pause before speaking the next sentence.)

I took both editorials to school in the morning. Ben Flescher, ever encouraging, said we could post them on the wall outside our classroom, one in the morning and the other in the afternoon. It certainly made me write every day. It also made me read the newspaper every day to look for stories and form opinions.

One of Dad's favourite sayings was "it's the truth that hurts," so that's what I called the editorial series. I wrote them for a few months before another opportunity presented itself.

In early 1972, Dad took me to the movie *Face-Off*, a Canadian production. It was a fictional story about a member of the Toronto Maple Leafs who falls in love with a pop singer. I was struck by the story and it was all I could think about. So I wrote my own version of *Face-Off*, creating a story about the floor hockey team for which I was playing goalie.

It was at the time when I started noticing young ladies. A girl at school named Brenda Andrews caught my eye. I wrote a story about going through our 20-game season and hanging around Brenda. In the story, my team—the Expos—won the provincial wheelchair floor hockey championship. I admit I copied the storylines of *Face-Off*, even the ending, having Brenda tragically die in a car accident. (Now I regret writing it that way, because I realize it wasn't really necessary, and was a little twisted.)

I wrote one version of the story, waited a few days and then wrote another draft. I wanted quantity, so I typed the story on half pages of paper—and that increased my page count to twenty-one.

Mom was my editor and was kind of impressed with the effort. Marion Northcot, who had helped us with the patterning, typed the manuscript, and she told me she cried at the ending. That was the first time I felt that my writing could evoke emotion.

I took my manuscript to school on a Monday. There was a horrible snowstorm on the Tuesday—so bad, in fact, that school buses were not running, so I spent the day at home. When I got to school the next day, I could not believe my eyes when I saw what was on my desk. Mr. Flescher, with the help of a few students who braved the snowstorm the previous day, had taken my twenty-one pages of copy to the school's Xerox machine and made twenty copies of the manuscript. Flescher designed a front cover with the name of the story—*A Goalie's Job*—and enlarged my school picture for the entire back cover.

It gave me a wonderful sense of accomplishment. More importantly, I think, it instilled great confidence that writing might be a very possible career for me.

I gave away so many books to family and friends that they were all gone within two weeks. Flescher ran off another twenty copies and frankly told me I would never make any money as an author if I kept giving my stories away. But I wasn't concerned about cash. I was just happy to be writing.

My first book (as a 13-year-old) came out in early February, and I felt I had another one in me before school ended in June. Glenrose had an annual Easter Tea in April and it was a feasible deadline to write another story. I discovered then how a deadline helped motivate me to get something written—something I used later in my three decades as a reporter and columnist with the *Edmonton Journal*.

My uncle Bill and aunt Dorothy enjoyed riverboating in northern Alberta and took me on a day trip down the Smoky River, just east of my hometown of Grande Prairie. The many flights from Edmonton to Philadelphia made me develop a deep love of airliners—and thankfully we were never in a crash. But I always wondered what that might be like, so that was my story: a plane leaving Grande Prairie headed to Edmonton, in a thunderstorm, that got hit by lightning and crashed into the Smoky

River—but was rescued by Uncle Bill and the rest of his riverboat friends the next day. I chose the name *Rescue!*, adding the exclamation mark to give it a little more zip.

As with what I could think of rather grandly as my first book, I wrote a first draft double-spaced on my IBM typewriter after my homework in the evening. Mom was again my first editor before I took it into school for Mr. Flescher and a few other teachers, who made grammatical and spelling corrections, but few editorial or story changes, something I found very encouraging. The second draft, typed in half-page size by neighbour Judy Harvey, came out to forty-eight pages, more than double the size of *A Goalie's Job*. My aunt Maxine, who was a wonderful painter, drew a picture of a cabin on an island in the middle of a river, which was the back page of the book.

Flescher loaded up the manuscript to take to the Xerox machine in the basement, gearing up to make a staggering 100 copies, which he said we'd need, since I'd arranged to sell them for twenty-five cents a copy at the Easter Tea, with all of it going to the union. (Okay, I wasn't the sharpest negotiator.) He was right— they were all sold before the Easter Tea ended.

I felt great… again. There aren't many feelings that beat having a book in your hand with your name on it. But it was about to get even better.

The night before the annual Glenrose awards day, Ben Flescher called Mom to say she might want to consider attending. He didn't say why, just that there was something coming down the pipe. Mom dressed me in a mauve shirt and white tie with my favourite pair of sneakers, and away we went. So my mom was there to see me presented with the school's citizenship award.

Did I need the award? Probably not, although I was proud to receive it. But it taught me a valuable lesson: if you want to make things happen, you have to initiate them, create your own opportunities, keep dreaming—but do some legwork to keep those dreams alive.

Of course, writing wasn't all I did. There was also that little detail called school and the work required to get through it. And, with early teen hormones stirring, I noticed in the very next classroom an eighth-grader named Cathy Frigon. She had long brown hair and was on a stretcher bed because she had curvature of the spine, a medical term for a sideways curve in one or more segments. It is also known as scoliosis. Cathy had surgery to correct her spine, and after she could sit up, she wore a brace for a month. She could walk slowly but could not turn her neck. But she stole my heart and gave me a kiss on the cheek one Thursday at 1:14 p.m. in the Glenrose library. I was in heaven.

Cathy was also my very first date. Someone gave me tickets to a boxing match at an inner city sports club on a Saturday night and Dad drove us. I realize now it wasn't a very romantic setting and we didn't watch much of the fight—I just wanted to be with Cathy. Life, in fact, was pretty much perfect—but remember what I said about Snakes 'n' Ladders?

* * *

I went into Grade 8 with a great deal of confidence in my writing and was planning to write another small book about the Little League all-star team I followed that summer. But I almost stopped writing altogether because of my homeroom teacher.

His name was Dave Wright. The 1972–73 school year was his last one before he retired. Wright was a freelance writer himself and offered to help me with my stories. In fact, he was one of the teachers who helped edit *Rescue!* He told me from the outset he was going to offer constructive criticism, and I was okay with that. I felt as a writer I could learn a great deal from such an approach.

But I think Mr. Wright went overboard with his criticism. He never offered much encouragement, if any. He also encouraged one of my best friends, Cam Tissington, to write a story to give me some competition. "Someone has to put you in your place," he kept saying.

Wright told me I should not be so competitive in baseball and floor hockey at Glenrose, that it would never get me a job and that I needed to focus more on my studies. Yet, when I gave him a new story—even a few pages—he was harsh and critical.

I was not a professional writer. I was a thin, 13-year-old, peach-fuzzed eighth-grader trying to develop my craft, and I was being shot down in so many ways that I gave up on the baseball story I was writing. I was tired of being told I was no good and could never become a writer. It was so discouraging, I didn't even write a word. Wright seldom taught anything from the textbooks. He let us play games or do anything we wanted. In a sense, the inmates were clearly running the asylum.

Mind you, he did do some great things, particularly for my class-mate, Derrick Coles, whose cerebral palsy made it very difficult for him to make himself understood when he spoke. Wright had served in the air force in World War II and was familiar with Morse code. He set up a station beside Derrick's desk so Derrick could tap out Morse code, and posted the Morse alphabet on the blackboard so every student could see it. Derrick memorized it and soon knew it like the back of his hand. Whenever he wanted to say something, he tapped it out and we could understand him perfectly. It was a great source of independence for him, all thanks to Dave Wright.

In the end, he did write on my report card that I passed into Grade 9. Still, he took a shot at my love of playing goaltender in floor hockey. "Cam needs to be reminded there is more than one goal," he wrote. I considered that to be a low blow—but always remembered it years later whenever I wrote a hockey story for the *Journal*.

I think I got the last word.

6
...

Ahead of Our Time

Wheelchair floor hockey was the school's sport. We
played it every noon hour in the gymnasium on the
main floor. For a while it was something special, a
bunch of kids with disabilities hanging out in the gym playing
pickup ball. And then the hand-wringers screwed it up.

Like Dad, I played goal. We began when I was seven years old.
Dad put me on my knees in between the kitchen table legs and
gave me Mom's potato masher as my goal stick. (Don't laugh at
my potato masher. That Gretzky kid used his grandma's legs as
goalposts, and he didn't turn out too badly.)

Over the years the game moved into the basement, with
neighbourhood guys coming after school to shoot tennis balls at
me. For my eighth birthday, Dad got me a set of goal pads, a chest
protector and a net.

I loved playing goal. When I first started at Glenrose, I fit
into the floor hockey program like a goal glove. There were some
funny looks when I got out of my wheelchair and crept to the goal
on my knees, but what did they know? When I put on my equipment, I was Ken Dryden with Team Canada, Johnny Bower with

the Leafs, or whatever super goalie I felt like being that day. It was glorious.

We were a motley crew, many kids playing in their wheel-chairs. Some of my best defencemen were in power wheelchairs and rolled back and forth to block shots, which had its draw-backs. The chairs often blocked my view. Often I was run over by my own team's chairs.

Many kids who didn't use wheelchairs wanted to play. So, like kids using jackets for bases in vacant lots, they figured it out, using chairs with castors on the four legs and propelling them-selves forward or backwards with their feet. That way kids who walked but had various disabilities—arthritis, hemophilia, or early stages of muscular dystrophy—could play and be part of a team. There's no way I can express what that meant to them.

In 1973 an all-star team was chosen for an exhibition game with nearby Spruce Avenue School. I managed to make it as the backup goalie. We had two forward lines, two sets of defencemen and two goalies. Our phys ed teacher, John Walters, was our coach. We could barely contain our excitement.

This wouldn't be just another pickup game amongst ourselves. We were a team representing our school. Maybe other schools had basketball or football—but we had floor hockey. In the seven years I attended Glenrose, I never felt school spirit so high. We weren't thinking of groundbreaking or social significance. We just wanted to line up and play. But, in truth, the exhibition games were a terrific form of integration between students with disabilities and without disabilities. The other team's players were not disabled. No problem! They played in the chairs with castors.

On the day of our first game, teachers let players out of our morning classes fifteen minutes early so we could have a good half hour before the game, which started at 12:15 in a gymnasium that was packed ten minutes before faceoff. We played well, and won 4–1. The Spruce kids demanded a rematch. Better still, make it best of three.

"Bring it on!" we cried. They did, and we beat them again, 3–0.

But something else was happening. Word was getting around that the Glenrose team was accepting challenges from high school teams to play floor hockey. I was following a Little League team in the west end and our coach, Brian Wilkes, was in Grade 12 at Jasper Place Composite High School. We arranged a game between Glenrose and JP, and I sure looked like a fool: JP was good, and soundly beat us 5–3, to give us our first loss.

We were getting more calls from Edmonton high schools asking to come play us. We even started talking about maybe forming a wheelchair floor hockey league with other schools in the city for the next year. Coach Walters intensified our practices so we could become even better. The spirit of competing was absolutely wonderful. Many of our teachers who made it very clear they were not sports fans in the least gave up their card game in the staff room to come cheer us on. Kids who couldn't play were our biggest cheerleaders, making signs and giving us great support.

It was amazing. And then, just like that, it was over.

Walters called a team meeting in his basement office. We knew from his expression that something was wrong. Then he laid it on us.

The Glenrose administration had called a special meeting at which it was decided it was wrong to have other schools come in and play floor hockey against us. Wrong!

There are expressions that cover their thinking. "A camel is a horse designed by a committee" comes to mind. But there's a better one: "These guys could screw up a one-car funeral."

These deep thinkers thought other schools were taking advantage of us. Why, the public might see it as the poor crippled kids being beaten at a game, and that was wrong, wrong, wrong.

The rest of the games were cancelled that day.

With one ill-conceived burst of stupidity, the deep thinkers robbed us of school spirit. Even worse, they ended a terrific form of integration between kids with disabilities and kids who didn't have them but could come to better understand the one vital fact that had to be accepted before anything could change—that kids with disabilities were just kids who happened to have disabilities.

Given the opportunity, sport can do that. We were proving it. But, no! Put us back in the fishbowl for everyone to take a good look at us—but, for God's sake, don't interact with us. My dad was fuming when I told him. "What a bunch of bullshit!" he said, which summed it up pretty nicely.

Yes, I know it was back in 1973, when the disability awareness movement hadn't gotten organized and our forecast was cloudy with little change. But a glorious opportunity to do some groundbreaking work to integrate us with students from all over Edmonton was missed because people who could have gotten behind us chose to do the easy thing.

The only solace I can take from this is that we were ahead of our time. Maybe it gave us more fight.

7

Cornstarch and Windsor Knots

On a warm Edmonton evening in late June 1973, Brian Wilkes leaned over to whisper in my ear.

"Send him," Brian said. "Send him to second."

Very slowly I moved my right hand over and touched my left elbow. The runner on first base touched the top of his batting helmet.

"Good. He got it," said Brian.

So let me fill in the blanks: top of the fifth inning, 2–2 tie, third game of the best of three for the Little League senior baseball league championship, ages thirteen to fifteen. And me? I'm sitting in my chair at the end of the players' bench on the third base-line—giving signals to baserunners.

It was Brian's brainwave as coach of the Village Esso team I had followed all season long. We were pretty good, finishing in first place, but we were in tough in the final against a team sponsored by Safeway. Heading into that deciding game, Brian felt that the Safeway club had figured out our signals, which could be a major problem. But he had an idea. He sat the team down in left field before the game and gave them his marching orders.

"Cam is giving the signals today," Brian said in his raspy coach's voice. "He'll be sitting right beside me at the end of the bench. I want you guys to look at me and I'll be giving you nothing but garbage signals. Pay no attention. Watch Cam. He will be giving you the bunt sign and the steal sign. Look at me, but keep your eyes on Cam."

Then, as the rest of the team did their stretches, Brian and I huddled. He said we were going to keep things really simple— bunt was hitting the left brow of my cap; steal, hit my left elbow twice.

"Screw this up, Tait," Brian said with his mischievous grin, "and we'll send you to the minors for the rest of your career."

What a wonderful feeling of being a part of the team, with something important to do, not just sitting at the end of the bench, cheering and swatting away mosquitoes. I was giving signals.

It always was important to me that if I was wearing a uniform—and I was—I wanted to contribute. I am forever grateful that Brian gave me the opportunity. I sent four runners to steal second base. All were safe. Brian just looked over at me and smiled.

In the end we won the game 5–3. We had just finished shaking hands when I saw Safeway's coach waving his hands at Brian. Then he raised his voice. Then he called the umpire over.

Brian told us to go back and pack up the equipment while he took care of things. We did. A few minutes later he came back to the bench, trying like hell not to laugh.

"The other coach said we cheated," he told us. "He said we changed our signals. I said we didn't. Then he asked who was giving them. I just smiled.

"And then he said: 'It was the crippled kid. You had the crippled kid giving your base signals. You cheated. This game is under protest.'"

Fat chance. The protest went absolutely nowhere. We were league champions.

● ● ●

Baseball swung into my life when I was seven. Dad bought me a brown plastic bat and white plastic ball, and he pitched to me. Underhand, of course. I was sitting on my haunches and managed to cut not a bad swing with my arms. Dad threw nice and slow, encouraging me to work on my timing for the hit, which I quickly figured out. Within a few days I had my first hit—and then hopped around the living room like a rabbit, aiming for the chesterfield, which was, in my mind, first base.

Later we took the game outdoors to the backyard. I was more fascinated with baseball uniforms than my ball and bat. When my mother learned of this, she went out and bought me a pair of New York Yankee pinstriped pajamas. But she said I could only wear them for bed, and not in the backyard when I was batting on my knees.

"The material is very thin," Mom said. "You will wear holes right through the knees if you crawl on the grass with them."

I didn't like the idea. But then, one summer afternoon, Mom had to go out for an hour and we had a babysitter. I had three of my friends over to play with me. There was my chance.

I convinced the babysitter to change me into my baseball pajamas and then went out to take the first pitch. I connected a hot grounder between second and third base and hopped on my hands and knees to first base. Of course, I was safe.

I looked down at my white uniform. Sure enough, there was a huge grass stain just below the knee. But I figured I would get the babysitter to wash the uniform right after the game. Mom would never know. Perfect.

I made it all the way from third base to home. Just as I placed my right hand on the bag that served as home plate, I heard a rip. I looked down at my right pant leg. It was torn. Post-game pajama-washing wasn't going to work.

That wasn't the only time Mom was left shaking her head about my baseball antics. I really liked seeing white lines down the first and third baselines. We needed them in the backyard on our diamond. Darn right, we did.

Poor babysitters. Mom had another afternoon appointment, so we had a babysitter, and a baseball game. Right before the game I asked the babysitter to reach in the cupboard above the stove for Mom's cornstarch.

"Take it outside and pour it on the grass," I said. "We have to make white lines on the baseball diamond."

For some reason, he did as I'd asked. But, be damned if we didn't run out of cornstarch a foot before we reached first base. The babysitter, bless his soul, put the empty box back in the cupboard. A few days later, Mom wanted to make biscuits and was dumbfounded as to where the cornstarch went.

I confessed. And was sent to my room—with a new pair of pajamas.

I knew my future in baseball—if I wanted one—wouldn't be as a player. I was just too damn hard on uniforms. But little did I know, the sport would teach me some of life's most important lessons.

Maybe our neighbour George McAvoy saw something in me. He helped with patterns in the evenings and coached a Little League team sponsored by Inland Cement. He suggested I become the team mascot, and threw in a bonus: my own uniform—a red and white uniform, just like the one worn by the St. Louis Cardinals major league team I loved watching on

Okay, I couldn't play the game I loved, but I had a great career as mascot, starting in 1968 with a team sponsored by Inland Cement.

television. A top, pants, socks and, of course, a cap. I was in! It rained on the evening I got it, but I was so excited I asked my mother if she would change me into it and, maybe, drive around the neighbourhood, visiting people to show off my new duds. Mom agreed, and off we went—in the rain.

What was the big deal for me to have a uniform? It was being accepted and being a part of the team. I was no longer the kid in the wheelchair who sat behind the backstop with the players' parents. Dammit, I was on the team. I sat on the end of the team bench and was included in the pep talks. Then, after one game, McAvoy pushed me across the diamond to shake hands with the other team.

Forgive me if I sound like a broken record, but being one of the boys meant the world to me. After all, I had the uniform to prove it.

Our team wasn't exactly setting Little League on fire in Edmonton, but we had fun. The team to beat was Overpass Equipment, who went on to win the league championship. Overpass was coached by Hugh Berry, who, just by chance, went to the same church our family attended, Trinity United. His wife, Marg, helped once a week with patterns. Coach Berry and I started a friendly rivalry after the baseball season whenever we saw each other at church. I don't think God minded too much.

Shortly before the next baseball season—the summer of 1969—George McAvoy said he would not be returning as coach. I mentioned this to Hugh Berry one Sunday at church. He leaned back on his heels, put his hands in his pockets and then made a pretty tempting offer: would I like to be the Overpass mascot?

I had one condition before I agreed to the transaction. "Do I get a uniform?" I asked.

He roared with laughter. "I think we can work something out," he said.

Deal.

Hugh Berry's son, Bill, was in high school and was a hell of a pitcher. He helped his father as an assistant coach. Bill and I really connected, and he shared some of his baseball strategy during games. Overpass had a great team—pitching, hitting and defence. Berry, a seasoned baseball and hockey player, was a fierce competitor; yet, he could harness his strong will to win to teach 11- and 12-year-old boys the basics of baseball. He quietly stirred my own competitive spirit—something, I think, that served me well throughout my life. When I think back, it's amazing what I was learning at the age of 10.

Mr. Berry was very good to me. We had a game one Sunday afternoon during two scheduled patterns. Mom and Dad broke the rules very few times to miss one pattern because of special circumstances. But two? Nope, they said. Couldn't do that. I was so disappointed—okay, pouting—that I would miss a few innings, I decided I wasn't going to go at all. All or nothing, man.

Just as I was finishing my crawling exercises after the second pattern, Mom said a green Ford station wagon pulled up in our driveway.

"It's Mr. Berry," she said. "And it looks like he brought the whole team with him."

I hopped up onto the chesterfield that was snug against the wall and looked out the window. Mom was right. The coach got out of the car and so did two players who were sitting in the front seat. Another five came out of the back seat. And another four climbed out of the very back of the station wagon—all in their uniforms and gloves.

"We brought the team bus," Berry said of his green wagon, a term that stuck for years later. "We missed you at the game so I thought we would come say hi."

And it was a happy group because the team had won 6–2 that afternoon. So, what would anyone do if their baseball team came over to their house? Take everyone to the backyard and have an impromptu baseball game, right? Yup, that's exactly what we did. The team stayed only fifteen minutes, but it meant so much to me that they'd come to see me.

We won the league championship, and it was the first time I felt the wonderful sense of success—and victory. I won a first-place ribbon in a church picnic three-legged race with my mother. But, uh, we kind of cheated. See, all Mom did was push me in my chair and—be damned—we crossed the finish line before anyone else.

But winning with Overpass was so special because it was a team effort. I remember the excitement on the bench late in June 1969 when the last out was made. We started slapping each other on the back, hugging each other and throwing our caps in the air.

Winning may be great. But perhaps even greater is sharing it with the people who got you there. We had a team party at the community hall—hot dogs, pop and ice cream. What struck me was the closeness of the players and realizing that we had won a championship. And we did it together.

In the middle of the hall sat the championship trophy—a little golden baseball bat and ball sitting on a piece of dark wood. A few months after we won the championship, Hugh Berry phoned one evening. Every player on the team was getting the trophy for a day, including me.

"I'm putting together a schedule and I wanted to know what day you would like it," he said over the phone.

I couldn't wait for the day to come when I had the trophy. I called as many friends as I could to come over and see it. Damn right, I was proud. Sure I never got a hit or made an out, but still, I was a part of the team. Hell, I had the uniform to prove it. And speaking of my uniform, Mom dressed me in it and took a few pictures of me in the backyard with the trophy.

I felt like a champion. I knew the feeling at a very young age, but I was also learning, very slowly, what it took to have an impact in what I wanted to do.

Hugh Berry gave me a great foundation for what lay ahead.

I was thirteen for the 1972 baseball season and that meant I was old enough for the senior division of Little League. Mr. Berry had quit coaching that year, but he introduced me to Jack Bottrell, whose son Randy, also my age, played for a team called Village Esso. Mr. Berry suggested I be the mascot for Village Esso. And yes, it came with a uniform. Done deal.

We were a young team and we struggled, finishing fourth in a four-team league. But we made the playoffs, only to be squished— and I do mean squished—by the first-place team called Oil Patch. They were coached by a man named Cec Papke, a junior hockey coach in the Western Canada Hockey League, who was working in the oil patch in the 1970s. He lived in Elmwood, a few neighbourhoods to the southwest of us.

He had kind of a nasal voice when he yelled instructions to his players, and it slowly turned into a fierce battle cry. I didn't know him well but knew he was a winning coach. And win he did: Oil Patch ended up winning the league championship.

Oil Patch was presented the trophy at the end of June. If you celebrated the league championship, that meant you got to pick an all-star team that would compete against other areas of the city, and, if you were really, really lucky, you had a shot at competing in the Little League World Series in Williamsport, Pennsylvania. I liked the sound of that challenge.

Mom called Coach Papke to see if I could be the team's mascot. Even though I couldn't hear his response over the phone, I could tell he wasn't jumping with joy. But still he said I could be part of the team. He was a taskmaster and wanted his team to be ready. Papke had two weeks before our first game and scheduled two practices a day: 9:15 a.m. and 3:00 p.m. Mom said she would drive me to Jubilee Park—a five-minute ride from our house.

Coach Papke shook everybody's hand the first morning, had all the players grab a seat in the bleachers, and then set the bar. "You guys are good. You might be the best group of young players I have worked with," he said. "In fact, you're so good, you're going to Thunder Bay, Ontario, to represent western Canada."

Okay. We hadn't even taken the field for practice, but dammit, we were going to Thunder Bay. I liked the way he thought.

And one more thing, he said. The team would travel by plane to Thunder Bay. "All of you guys have to wear a tie on the plane," he ordered. "Because when you look good, you feel good—and you do good. So I want all of you guys to tie your own ties."

Challenge accepted. I couldn't wait for Dad to come through the back door after work that day. When he did, I hit him with my question: "Dad, can you teach me how to tie a tie?"

He muttered something under his breath. "Are you crazy?" he asked.

"No," I said. "Our baseball coach said we have such a good team that we're going to the national championships in Thunder Bay. On the airplane. And we all have to tie our own tie, and since I am part of the team..."

Dad looked skyward. "This may be the craziest thing I have ever heard, you tying a tie with your hands," he said. "Tell you what. I'll show you three times and three times only. Then, you're on your own."

Dad undid the tie he was wearing and slowly showed me how to tie a double Windsor knot. Single? No way. Had to be a double. And then it was up to me.

Every day after our afternoon practice, I went to Dad's tie rack, selected a tie and started tying. And tying. And tying. I spent an hour a day trying to figure this damn thing out.

The days turned into a week. I came up with more knot configurations than the Royal Canadian Navy and Boy Scouts had in both of their manuals. But was there a knot I could proudly wear with a crisp starched shirt? Not a chance.

Then, on the twelfth day, I don't know what I did, but everything seemed to go where it was supposed to, and my knot was just perfect. But was it a fluke? So I grabbed another one of Dad's ties and attempted to produce another knot. I did. I had an hour before Dad came home from work. I untied all of his forty-seven ties hanging from the rack and re-tied them before he walked through the door.

Mission accomplished. More importantly, I was ready to travel with the team.

I tied my first tie two days before our first game. I really wasn't looking forward to the start of tournament play, because I was learning so much from Papke's two-a-day workouts. I paid special attention to how he had three, sometimes four, drills going on at once so every player was involved. Papke had three assistants—Gordie Murray, Dean Coquette and Willie Nielsen—run drills, and he circled around to everyone. And what really struck me was how he always stopped to teach something new in the drill and walked away to the next one, clapping his hands and leaving words of encouragement.

I thought I knew baseball fairly well as a 13-year-old kid. But Coach Papke taught me so much about the fundamentals of hitting, fielding and pitching. I sat and soaked in as much as I could when he had the team practise baserunning, bunting, double steals and squeeze plays. He demanded perfection, and if the players didn't do it right, dammit, he made them do it over until they did. I was taught that during the patterning treatment, but hearing it from someone outside of the treatment was very enlightening.

Coach Papke was friendly to me, shook my hand and said hello every time he saw me. But he never wheeled me up to the bench for a fireside chat. I often wondered if he really understood I was learning a great deal from him.

He did have my back, though. The team met before every game. One day, just as we were finishing up, the biggest swarm of bees I have ever seen circled around the bench. Everyone ran like hell, including Papke, and jumped the wire fence. Me? I was left there, trying to pedal backwards to get away from the bees.

"Holy shit. We forgot Cam," Papke said after the mayhem settled down. "I'll go get him."

He came running and then pushed me to safety.

He had a line for everything—too many to repeat. But there's one I'll never forget. Brian Grandfield was one of our starting pitchers, but he had a rough day at a practice. Papke walked out to the mound to settle Grandfield down. We could hear him as clear as day.

"Brian, if you are a pitcher, then my asshole is a machine gun," he barked.

The night before our first game of the double knockout, we had a team meeting and hot dogs at Mr. Papke's. I had to go because that was the night he was handing out uniforms. They were beautiful—white, red and black. We were the Edmonton Falcons. And we were all pretty impressed at the price tag—$44 per uniform. Back in 1972 we thought that was a hell of a price for uniforms. But we looked good, and we'd earned them.

The double knockout tournament began July 15 and we breezed through our first three games. We lost our fourth, and it gave me a lesson I'll always remember. The team was pretty confident going into the game, even cocky. Coach Papke stressed how important it was to have a really good infield warm-up. Get a good feel for the ball. Snap it around the bases. Feel good about yourself before the first pitch.

But that night the pre-game warm-up was a disaster. Throws were wild. Balls were dropped. The guys did not look ready at all. Papke looked angry and concerned as he quickly came back to the dugout and summoned the team to the left-field fence. Nobody pushed me over to the impromptu meeting, but I could hear his displeasure from where I sat.

We lost that game, and maybe some of our confidence. To this day I think of that game and the importance of getting ready for everything. We did bounce back in the final, and had a 5–3 lead late in the game. We started talking about winning and representing Edmonton in Calgary, and then we'd be off to Thunder Bay.

We lost 7–5, and we never got to fly to Thunder Bay.

But, damn, I still can tie a tie.

8
. . .

Back to Class

Meanwhile, back in the classroom...

We entered Grade 9 and it was a breeze. I am a little miffed to this day that we weren't pushed more, especially since it was our chance to enter high school with a good, concentrated work ethic.

One teacher, an older woman, often would stroll into class a good fifteen minutes late because she "was having such a good time chatting in the staff room." Maybe she did. But what was that doing for our education? Not much.

Ben Flescher returned to teach us math, but unfortunately, he couldn't control some of my classmates who now were well into their teens, some of them a little angry and bitter at life. Flescher wheeled up to one student who had a question about math but instead asked, "Do you have venereal disease?"

Flescher was a meek and mild man, and really should have sent the student to the principal's office for a stern talking-to. Sadly, he just took it and did nothing. Maybe he couldn't. Still, it was a huge sign of disrespect and I am very sad it happened. I can't help but wonder if it was yet another sign of the teaching staff thinking we didn't have much of a future after Grade 12, so why bother instilling social skills like respect and good manners?

Me, I always knew something would be there for me after Grade 12—I just didn't know what it would be. I think I got that from the continual encouragement I got from all our friends and neighbours who helped us with the Philadelphia program. Other kids, sadly, did not have that support.

But then, there was Jack Hassan, who taught Grade 9 science and, we already knew, would be our homeroom teacher in Grade 10.

Hassan was very serious about what he taught and didn't merely ask a good effort from us, he demanded it. That alone kept us on our toes and sharp. Right away, we knew who was boss. Let someone show up late for class and he'd stop whatever he was saying and stare at the miscreant in dead silence until textbooks were on the desk. Before long, we were arriving five minutes before the start of science class and making sure that our books were out by the time Hassan walked into class.

Years later, working for the *Journal*, I always tried to be five minutes early for an interview. Given good teachers, the lessons stick.

My marks going into tenth grade were above average, but I struggled with the jump to high school, especially the workload that would potentially lead to a high school diploma.

Hassan was, indeed, our homeroom teacher, and high school didn't change his approach. At the top of the blackboard, in big red letters, he gave us the main rule: IF YOU DO NOT UNDERSTAND, ASK! That was encouraging, but I was struggling with two subjects he taught—math and biology. They didn't inspire me and I didn't work very hard at them. Bad move. Hassan gave me a final grade of 45 percent on a biology project that involved planting some wheat, watching it grow and keeping notes. Be still, my beating heart.

I did worse in Math 13, a modified version of Math 10, which was needed for university. On a geometry exam I got 4 percent. Four percent! I mean, I was using an electric typewriter and used the "/" and "_" characters on the keyboard to illustrate my answers. It was hard. Damn hard.

Hassan suggested I switch to the Math 15 course, which was geared toward a business approach. He also suggested we use calculators to make things easier. My grade improved, but not my enthusiasm. I wasn't sure what I'd be doing for a living, exactly, but I knew it wouldn't include business mathematics. Fortunately, there was Pauline Kachuk, who was known for her love of English and literature. She taught us English for three years through high school, and her enthusiasm really inspired me to think about writing stories again.

Many of my friends away from Glenrose played hockey, the best of them leaving home at fifteen to play for junior teams in other towns. That really fascinated me, especially hearing the words from Cec Papke talking about his 15-year-old son, Hal, leaving home to play hockey. "It's time he became a man," Papke said in his gruff voice.

Hockey was such a big love of my life. I would have given anything to have the opportunity to go on a junior hockey journey. I imagined what it felt like and could almost smell the exhaust fumes when I thought about getting on the team bus after a road game. The more I thought about it, the more determined I was to put it into print.

I created a fictional eight-team junior hockey league throughout Alberta and Saskatchewan with a lead character playing for a team in North Battleford—an area I knew well from our family summer holidays. I added a girlfriend and an elderly gentleman with a personality like Uncle Bob, someone I really admired. And, of course, lots and lots of hockey. Then, armed with a relatively new electric typewriter, a stack of yellow copy paper and my eight-track stereo player (I found listening to music helped my creative process), I got to work.

Mom and Dad had built a work area for me in the basement, on one condition: homework—all of it—first, hockey second. First fact, then fiction. I'd begin the book project about 7:30 p.m. Sometimes Mom called down to me at eleven to tell me to come up to bed. I lost track of time when I wrote, and it was really hard to obey my mother—especially when I was in the middle of writing details about a hockey game with the score tied 3–3.

I felt great freedom when I was writing fiction and loved steering the story the way I wanted it to go. Maybe it was the sense that I could control something when I had trouble controlling so many other things in my life. It had been two and a half years since I had written my last story and I was really noticing my creativity increasing. I had always been told quality is better than quantity, but still had great pride when I rolled a sheet of yellow paper in my typewriter for my one-hundredth page.

The story ended hours after the seventh game of the league championship final, with the hero and his girlfriend going for a walk in a light snowfall. The North Battleford team did not win. That would be a storybook ending, and for most of us, life doesn't end that way. I wanted my story to be about the journey and people giving it all they have. Some are fortunate to capture championships, but most of us don't. Yet, the things we learn along the way are priceless. That was the message I wanted to get across.

Mom helped me compile the 121 double-spaced pages I had typed to take into school. Mrs. Kachuk had said she'd be pleased to edit the manuscript, but warned that she wasn't that much of a junior hockey fan. The day I gave her the story was a day we had an exam on Shakespeare. I looked up from my exam every ten minutes or so to see if she was enjoying the story. She made a few notes and then she looked at me. She didn't say a word; she just smiled. And that must have happened ten times during the class. That smile was all I needed. It just felt so good to be writing again.

I rewrote the entire story, the first copy to the left of my typewriter as I retyped every word, expanding the story as I went, adding a few more twists and turns to the plot and really getting into it. I could feel the excitement of the game, smell the fresh popcorn that was made in the lobby between periods and feel the pains and bruises after the game on a four-hour bus ride home. After the book was printed, people asked me who the main character was. I said I didn't know, but a few years later, I admitted it was really me. I was living my dream of playing junior hockey through writing it.

Mom contacted one of her friends from the Peace River country, Roy Gouchey, to see if he had any ideas about getting my manuscript printed. Mr. Gouchey taught school at Victoria Composite High School and said he could have it done on the school's printing press. One of his students, Marion Campbell, volunteered to type the manuscript for the press. And in June 1975, Gouchey delivered five boxes of my new book, *The Whistle Blows*, complete with a heavy cover illustrated with an ice surface lined as a hockey rink. It had 108 pages and I had a new pen name: C.D. Tait. Proud? Oh, yeah.

Mom suggested I sell the book for a dollar a copy. The first call I made was to Cathy Frigon, who had stopped going to Glenrose three years earlier. But I was still pretty sweet on her. She invited me over that day and said she wanted three books. I was in love all over again.

Between friends and family and people at Glenrose, we were out of the first hundred books within two weeks. (Or so I thought. Mom managed to hide ten copies from me because I was selling them to anyone I could.) Now I had $87 for my summer spending money.

I felt a much greater sense of accomplishment with *The*

Whistle Blows. It seemed my creativity had reached a new level and my ability to tell a story was getting better. The only constructive criticism people were sharing with me was that it read like an account of somebody's year in hockey—like a newspaper story—rather than a book. I think about that often and wonder if that was when my newspaper tenure was starting to take form.

Roy Gouchey said he could do a second run and we printed another two hundred copies. I think I have one left.

9.
• • •

Maybe If I Study . . .

I was an average student but I certainly wasn't any screaming hell. Mom made a great point over the summer just before I went into Grade 11. Maybe if I applied myself to my schoolwork the same way I'd done on the hockey book, I would see results. I used the foundation and work ethic for *The Whistle Blows* for my homework, and much to my surprise, I was enjoying it.

Helen Wilinski was our homeroom teacher and was specifically a typing teacher. I was forming strong beliefs that I would probably be making my living writing something; I had not figured out what type of writing, but a good typing speed would be an asset. Pauline Kachuk was such a joy to learn English from and she made me a big fan of Shakespeare—something my dad had enjoyed in high school. Mrs. Frost taught a psychology class, and I really enjoyed learning about the study of people. Having so many volunteers around me when I was a boy may have cultivated my love of people. But this school thing was working—maybe because both sides were working at it.

And then, suddenly, the old radio news enthusiasm flared up

again, naturally at 630 CHED, radio home of my mentor, Eddie Keen.

In January 1976, fellow student and bus-mate Brenda Currey had some news. Her father, Dick, knew Gary Bridger, one of the weekend newsmen. Did I want to tour the CHED newsroom with her and her dad? The tour was all it took. The tension of deadlines, the old teletype machines clanking off wire stories and the constant telephone calls with news tips fascinated me. Just like that, I wanted to be a newsman.

During our tour, I'd met news announcer Randy Kilburn. We struck up a friendship, which I may have strained by becoming a pest. I started phoning him every day in the CHED newsroom, asking him questions about the lead story, what interviews he had lined up and what other things he was working on, and inviting myself back to CHED another Saturday to meet and watch him work.

After Randy read the 1:20 p.m. news headlines, he let me take the page of yellow paper, all in capital letters and double-spaced. I studied it for days, looking at the way it was written and the selection of news stories. I realized that I could never read news copy because of my voice, but maybe I could write it.

Now I had a goal. Time to go to work on it. After my homework was done that night, I tried my hand at writing news-ready copy, and timed the items by reading them silently to myself. My basement workroom became a fantasy radio newsroom. I wrote five newscasts in two hours—three at the top of the hour and two on the half hour. Mom, involved as always, cut out random stories from the *Journal* that I tried to rewrite into radio style. I still remember the rush I felt, getting a sample newscast written one or two minutes before my phantom deadline. It was something I felt I could do as a career.

Poor, patient Randy. He never had a chance. When we examined capital punishment in social studies, I wrote an essay on it, converted it to a sample radio piece, and asked Randy to read it for recording to a cassette tape. It was long—four and a half minutes—but it gave me great confidence in what I might be able to do. In one of my countless telephone calls, I asked him if radio stations specifically hired writers to write the news. He said no, news announcers wrote their own copy since they read it, which made sense. Then he suggested writing in the continuity department.

"What is that?" I asked.

Randy told me that's where radio commercials are written, and gave me the name of a young continuity writer at CHED named Daryl Hooke, who he said would be happy to help me. I often wonder if that was a nice way for Randy to divert my telephone calls to someone else.

I called Daryl the next morning and I could tell he was a little hesitant with my request, and my desire to write for radio.

"What grade are you in?" Daryl asked.

I told him. He said to call him when I was in Grade 12 and he would offer me some guidance. Okay, I'd wait. Meanwhile, I kept listening, writing news, and making notes. If—no, when—a chance came, I was going to be ready.

I got a lukewarm reception when I told my family and friends I wanted to be a writer for radio. Many rolled their eyes while others quickly changed the conversation. Although nobody openly admitted it, I could sense most everyone I shared my vision with thought I was completely off my rocker. Yet, I had a vision and a dream. I felt it had to be chased. My new work ethic was paying off. I graduated from Grade 11 with a 74-percent average, with my best subjects being English and psychology. All it had taken was maximum effort. Look out, radio. I'm coming.

A Great Lesson

Our Grade 12 class was small—Curtis, Derrick and me. To us, that wasn't surprising. Through seven years at Glenrose we'd watched too many classmates fall to an enemy they could neither see nor fight.

Muscular dystrophy was inexorable. We'd watched so many friends lose ground as they progressed through their teens, the disease weakening the muscles of the back, legs and lungs, often leading to the pneumonia that lowered their defences below the point of resistance. We'd been there with them as they faded, seen the empty desks, heard the choked and sorrowful announcements that another friend was gone.

Curtis had MD. I first met him in Grade 6, when he walked in under his own steam but grew weaker as the year progressed. Soon, his weakened back forced him into a wheelchair to get around. Sometimes he leaned over too far to one side and couldn't get back up. He'd ask for help, and Derrick and I would push his body back up to a sitting position.

We knew Curtis was getting weaker but we never talked about it. Never. I credit so much of that to Curtis for having the positive and downright courageous attitude he did. He never discussed past memories—he was too busy making new ones. He was a great sports fan and we used to talk about the days when we would both be reporters, he covering football, me on the hockey beat.

When Grade 12 rolled around, I was afraid that Curtis might not live to get his high school diploma and that scared the hell out of me. Grade 12 is where you start talking about all your hopes and dreams—family, careers, vacations and so much more. Somehow, the more people you have around you, the more the dream comes alive, the easier it is to push back the knowledge that the deck might be stacked. Many of my friends did not live long enough to go out on a date or to graduate. When I think back to school days, it's the memories of the ones we lost that surface most often. I owe it to them to keep looking to tomorrow.

Luckily, Curtis wasn't skinny like other kids with MD. He started using an electric wheelchair in high school and that was great mobility for him. Still, as time went by, we saw little signs that he was getting weaker. Mentally, I crossed my fingers. Ben Flescher returned as our homeroom teacher and that felt comfortable. Being disabled himself, he took some time in class to tell us what it was like as an adult living with a disability. He talked about housing, transportation and employment and told us it could very well be our biggest challenge and we had to work a little harder to prove ourselves.

I really don't know if we took it all that seriously. It was 1976. The disability movement was just getting rolling, but there really weren't many people with disabilities integrated into the work-force. Flescher was a role model for us because he was holding down a full-time job.

Looking back now, I knew I wanted to write for radio. But did I actually envision myself working for a mainstream radio station? Not really.

Mom was my first supporter in my radio dream when she called the Northern Alberta Institute of Technology because she heard they had a Radio and Television Arts program. She contacted the program head, Eric Candy, and explained my situation. Candy met me one morning at Glenrose to discuss the possibility of me taking RTA in the next year. He was very supportive of my desire to write for radio. He explained, though, that the course taught every aspect of broadcasting and said it would be very difficult for me to operate equipment like television studio cameras and take the announcer part of the course. But he said I could certainly take the broadcast writing course for television and radio.

Radio and Television Arts was a two-year program, but Candy said it would be pointless for me to attend NAIT for the entire two years. He would talk to the registrar, he said, about how we could make this work. We shook hands at the end of our meeting and I was confident I would be going to NAIT after Grade 12.

A few weeks later, I received a letter in the mail confirming that I had been accepted into Radio and Television Arts as a "special student" taking two writing courses on broadcast writing. I was ecstatic.

11

...

Getting Mainstreamed

There was another brighter reason why high school classes were small at Glenrose, and it was very exciting. Students with physical disabilities were being integrated into the mainstream school system. It began with kids with moderate disabilities who started their schooling at Glenrose, but within a year or so moved on to schools in their communities. As years passed, more kids with more severe mobility issues left.

I remember being happy for them about going to their home school—especially kids who were not from Edmonton and stayed at the Glenrose nursing unit throughout the school year. But I also felt a sense of loss on several levels. I had formed good friendships with many kids and to have them leave was difficult. I think it also hurt the overall school spirit, because as more and more kids were integrated, Glenrose was, sadly, getting smaller. There were times when I thought I'd been left behind. I really wonder now, if I would have had one more year of high school, would I have been attending Glenrose? I very well could have gone to Jasper Place Composite High School near our house.

Glenrose followed the same curriculum set out by the

Edmonton Public School Board for high school diplomas. We worked hard at our core subjects: English, social studies, typing and sociology (I had my math credits from Grade 11 so didn't have math to worry about), but it was the other "aimed-at-us" classes that provided the real education.

Glenrose had a truly impressive industrial arts laboratory located in the basement. It had everything: a darkroom, a print shop, hands-on equipment for courses in plastics, ceramics, woodworking and hydraulics. Derrick, Curtis and I had trouble operating much of the equipment, but

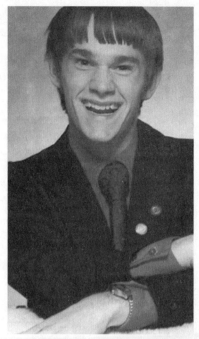

High school was a mixed bag for me, but by ninth grade I knew what I wanted to be. I would be a writer. I just didn't know where or what.

our teacher, Jake DeLeeuw was very good about teaching us how things worked and it was great for general knowledge.

Mr. DeLeeuw encouraged us to take on a project and then tell him what to do, step by step. I thought that was a tremendous teaching method in many ways. It taught us how to work with people and how to give instructions. Those lessons served me throughout my life during times when I couldn't do something myself, but could tell someone how to do it. This specifically helped me in directing my personal care in later years.

We had a class called PFL—Perspectives For Living (Curtis and I called it the Professional Football League)—aimed at teaching us several basic life skills that we could use after Grade 12. We caught a break in our teacher, Joyce Tipping, who was a very progressive thinker. The school hospital had an independent living suite with a living room, kitchen, bedroom and bathroom. The suite was accessible—lowered counters, grab bars in the bathroom and low light switches—and was designed as a trial suite for people who wanted to live on their own. Mrs. Tipping arranged for each of us to stay in the suite for three nights with Glenrose nursing staff assisting us with showering and dressing, and helping us with breakfast, and then with our nighttime care.

Each of us was given a budget to buy groceries for three days and took the Glenrose bus to go shopping. I loaded up on Coke, chips and very little real food. I got a failing grade on my shopping trip, but sure enjoyed what I did buy. The experience we gained from the living suite was a great sample of the type of living situation we could have. More and more, life's targets were looking reachable. But that was for later. Right then, only one thing mattered—the Senior Prom.

12

Prom Night

In March we started planning the graduation prom at the Edmonton Plaza (now the Westin Hotel) in downtown Edmonton. I had the great honour of being voted class valedictorian for the grad banquet, and really enjoyed writing my speech. Given the size of the grad class, the crowd wouldn't be more than about fifty (including two of my favourite people, Uncle Walt and Aunt Maxine, who drove up from Calgary), which put the grad speech what I now considered right up my alley: writing for the ear and making it conversational.

My date was Janet King, a wonderful girl I'd met in Grade 10 in a church youth group near our home. Janet looked absolutely stunning in a long white dress. She helped me walk into her parents' house, and I gasped when she opened a brown box and pinned a boutonniere on my lapel—a first for me. She then sat down beside me and gave me a graduation present from her and her parents—a very elegant pair of marble bookends.

She reached for my hand and squeezed it before looking me in the eye.

"This is your special day," she said. "Thank you very much for letting me be a part of it."

Beautiful girl holding my hand, boutonniere on my lapel, class valedictorian and a prom dinner at a posh hotel. Tait, old boy, somewhere you did something right.

We had several graduation parties in June, including one at our place with all the grads and our teachers. It was a great night for everyone except Mom. She brought in a case of beer for one of our guests, who unfortunately fell halfway up the steps and sprained her ankle. Mom always hated beer. We also had a party at Curtis' home in Lamont, a small town almost an hour north-east of town. He was doing great and looking forward to taking a business course in the fall. It was wonderful to see him with his family and to share their deep Ukrainian heritage. The party lasted until two in the morning, when we all sang "O Canada" before bidding everyone goodnight.

Curtis lived across the street from the town's baseball diamond.

"I wonder if we woke the neighbours by singing 'O Canada,'" Curtis said. "I hope they don't come out of their houses, thinking there's a ball game."

• • •

Again, time out.

We're about to leave Glenrose, as I did in 1977, and I don't want anyone thinking I left with nothing but bad memories. School was tough on me, but I probably handed back my share. And we did have fun, the kind of scrapes and near misses and madcap nonsense that is a part of every high-schooler's life.

For instance, there was the time my classmate, Owen Stewart, was without his power chair for a few days and we had to pull and push him all over the school. Owen had a very dry sense of humour and could be sarcastic at times. One afternoon, we had heard about enough. So, we pushed him into the women's staff washroom. And left him there, where he stayed until a teacher went to the washroom, found him and escorted him out.

But most of all, I want to talk about Jim Silverson.

Our friendship began in the middle of Grade 9. Jim worked as the lifeguard in the swimming pool that was used by patients in the rehabilitation hospital right next to the school, also called Glenrose.

"Ever try swimming?" he asked.

Well, yes, whenever our family went on holidays to British Columbia. Dad strapped a life jacket on me whenever we were near a lake, and I got on my back and swam backwards. I wasn't very good at it, but it was a great way to cool off after a hot day of driving in the car.

Jim kept offering me swimming lessons but I wasn't interested. But he finally got me into the pool in March 1974, one noon hour a week. The Glenrose pool was heated to 72°F and it really helped relax my muscles. Plus, I wasn't as spastic when I was in the water.

Jim was very good, and patient—at the beginning—letting me find my own comfort level swimming on my back. Since I had trouble keeping my head out of water, he would walk behind me with his hand under my neck as I swam. Once we figured that out, I worked on strengthening my arms and legs so I could increase my speed in the water. To my surprise I was getting better—and enthusiastic. When the school year ended, Mom drove me to the pool five days a week in the afternoons over the summer months. Jim had said he had a project for me in the fall and wanted me in the best possible shape.

I was in suspense until September, when he finally told me his idea. He wanted me to swim a mile. "Be good for you mentally as well as physically," he said.

I jumped at the idea. I was struggling a little with my

schoolwork, and swimming let me focus on something I could do, be decent at, improve my ability and take out some frustrations. Three noon hours a week, starting at 12:10, I swam for fifty minutes. Jim was a great cheerleader and was helping me with endurance.

One Friday I got to the pool earlier than normal. "If we hustle, we might be able to swim a half mile today," Jim said as he wheeled me down the ramp into the water.

"Let's do it," I said.

Jim had the physiotherapy department make me a neck brace out of Styrofoam to help steady my neck, and it really helped me a lot. I managed to swim thirty-six laps that noon hour—six more than I had ever swum before—which was half a mile.

"Good warm-up," Jim said, "Next week, you can shoot for the mile."

I had to clear it with Mrs. Wilinski, since my typing class went from 1:00 to 2:15 p.m. She said it was okay if I missed class, since this was a big undertaking. I swam every day and tried to get all the rest that I could in the days before the big event. The only thing worrying me was being able to swim twice the distance I'd done the previous week.

My cousins, Bob and Cathy Beattie, were in Edmonton the day I tried to swim the mile, and came to watch. It must have been pretty boring, watching me go around and around for seventy-two laps, which took me a little over two hours. But they hung in the whole way, and their support meant a great deal to me.

I could feel every muscle in my body running out of gas in the final lap. I finished on fumes, my legs so weak I couldn't prop myself up at the end of the pool. I had never been so drained in my life.

After I changed, somebody wheeled me up to the second floor for the last ten minutes of my typing class. I fell asleep at my desk.

Prom Night

I kept swimming and Jim said I was getting good—so good, in fact, that he entered me in the 100-metre race in the Alberta Cerebral Palsy Games at the University of Alberta pool, which, I discovered to my dismay, was ten degrees colder than the one at Glenrose. I was fearful that might make my muscles tighter, which would slow me down. Not so. I did alright and finished second.

All this happened because a lifeguard cared about a scrawny kid in a wheelchair. I will carry that memory always.

13
• • • •

Tait at NAIT

It took about twenty minutes on my first day at NAIT to realize that life as I had known it was over. It scared the hell out of me.

I had arrived confident that I could handle whatever the new school threw at me. Hadn't I won that $200 scholarship in Grade 12? Wasn't there a new electric typewriter on the way? Okay, Glenrose had been a segregated school and NAIT wasn't. But I felt I was pretty well adjusted and could relate to people quite well. Mom and Dad had gotten me involved with hockey, baseball and a church youth group in high school to let me interact with kids and adults who were not disabled. How different could this be?

Well, faster, for one thing, everyone rushing around with places to be and people to see. I felt like a 33-rpm record with everyone else spinning at 78. "Tait," I thought, "you're gonna have to change gears."

And then Eric Candy threw me the curve. I had two classes a week, he said, Thursday and Friday afternoons. I didn't have to turn up the rest of the week, but could if I really wanted to. The issue was where I could study at NAIT, but he said if I really wanted to come in, he would figure out something. Our meeting ended just before 9:30 a.m. on a Thursday and my courses didn't start for another week.

"You may as well go home and enjoy the rest of your day. And stay home tomorrow," he said. "If you want, come back Monday— but only if you want to."

Dad drove me home, and I was disappointed and a little bit lost. From the time I was five years old, my life had been totally structured, first by the patterning, then school and its timetable. But it wasn't even ten in the morning and I had nothing to do. It felt really weird, especially since Candy left me with the impression that my days at NAIT might not be very busy.

I understood that I only had two classes a week, but I wanted to go five days a week. I wanted to be around a radio environment and learn as much as I could. Was this a glimpse of my future?

Back at NAIT the following Monday, I had knots in my stomach, hoping I could stay the entire day and, more importantly, have something to do.

Mr. Candy said he had a place for me to work. He wheeled me into a small television studio that was being used for storage for the Radio and Television Arts department. The room contained two broken-down television studio cameras, a desk and my typewriter. He also brought some "fact sheets" from the NAIT radio station, containing all kinds of facts and figures on various charity groups in the city. "Use these and start writing thirty- and sixty-second commercials," he said. "It's what the students are doing and it will be good practice before you start taking the broadcast writing course on Thursday."

He'd made the effort, and I appreciated it. Now it was up to me.

My days were not what anyone would call action-packed. I'd arrive a little after 9:00, bid good morning to the broken-down cameras, and start writing. A few times a day, Candy would come

First step along the career path: broadcast writing course at the Northern Alberta Institute of Technology, here with classmates Ken Sellar, Greg Johnson and Cheryl Smith.

in to check on me, read some of my copy and bring me more fact sheets. The only other company I had were the two technicians who periodically popped in to try something new with the broken-down cameras. They'd open them with some fancy-looking tools, have a good look at the innards, stand back, take another good look, and another, then shake their heads in bewilderment and leave. Other than that I was left on my own to write.

Mom packed me a lunch that I took to the cafeteria. Most days, I sat by myself. A few kind students asked me to join them sometimes, but the conversation didn't last very long. One of the first questions they asked me was what technology I was on.

"Radio and Television Arts," I proudly answered.

"Oh, I see," they'd say, raising their eyebrows and maybe even rolling their eyes. I could see they didn't really take me seriously, which basically ended the conversation. I tried to keep it going but they quickly tuned me out and said they couldn't understand me.

I get that. There weren't many people with physical disabilities going to NAIT, and I was the first person in a wheelchair taking the broadcasting course. Perhaps it was up to me to do some public education at NAIT. When we took the same writing course together, I did meet the students who started the program at the same time I did, but that was only twice a week and there wasn't time to form solid friendships in that environment, because right after class I went back to my cubbyhole and shook my head at the broken-down cameras.

Every day, I made a visit into CHNR, the school's radio station, and could barely fit my wheelchair into the newsroom. It was clear my fellow students were still trying to get their heads around someone in a broadcasting course who could not be understood that well. I asked if I could post an editorial called "Cam's Corner" on a bulletin in the newsroom. I did it primarily to prove I could write and had a sense of news—and, indirectly, a way of proving myself through my writing.

It got better. A month into my stay, Candy found an empty office right beside the radio production studio at NAIT (back then, the RTA program was spread throughout the NAIT campus rather than being all together) and introduced me to several of the students who were taking the radio production lab then—Pat Peterson, Jerry Griffin and Gary Chomyn. Finally, I was starting to feel like part of my technology.

Gary was in his second year, and we quickly became friends. He checked into my new office almost every hour and we chatted. He invited me for coffee, wheeled me to the cafeteria for lunch and introduced me to other students, which was very helpful. But my new friends were still a little curious about what made me tick. They were always polite and said hello in the hallway but that was about it—until one Friday afternoon when we went for a beer after class at the Kingsway Inn, the same bar I went to when I celebrated my eighteenth birthday. We had a few laughs that night, and a few beers, and I warned them what would happen if I consumed too many—I'd walk a straight line.

That long night at the Kingsway Inn, I became one of the gang. I noticed it the very next Monday. A routine "Hi, how are you?" turned into "Cam, how was your weekend? Did you see the [Edmonton] Eskimo game?" NAIT was becoming my school.

14

On My Own

At 18 years old, I knew I had to get my own place. Sure, I could maintain the status quo, but I couldn't have it both ways, fighting at every level to live a normal life, but coming home every night to Mom and Dad. My own life aside, what kind of a life would that be for them? And with Dad retiring in the next ten years, I did not want to put any more limits on them than I already had.

There was, of course, the option taken by some of my Grade 12 classmates, who moved into nursing homes. I visited some of them after school, and the institutional setting sent shivers up my spine. There was no form of independence. Friends told me that when they wanted to sleep in on the weekends, they were awakened at seven in the morning by the janitors vacuuming their room. Meals were at a certain time, every day. Most of my friends shared a room with people three times their age.

No thanks.

But I knew I did not want to live at home with Mom and Dad as an adult. There was a danger to it. I'd become lazy at home because my folks were always there to help me, to do things for me that I should be finding ways to do for myself, and the longer I stayed, the easier it would be to snuggle down in this wonderfully warm cocoon and let people I loved wait on me. I needed to find my way to maximum independence, and soon.

There had to be another way, and I found it. Just after I started at NAIT, a quadriplegic high school friend, Jerry Schaffer, had moved into a new apartment complex in the west end, which included adaptive suites for people in wheelchairs. He secured government funding for apartment rent—back then it was $395 and $100 for food. Needing a live-in assistant, he made a deal with a friend. Jerry would pay the rent and utilities in exchange for personal care services. It worked like a damn, he said.

I had become good friends with Jerry Griffin, a 21-year-old in my technology classes who took enormous pride in smoking a pipe and wanted to move out of his parents' home. (Or maybe they wanted to get rid of the pipe smoke.) He was already working weekends at a group home for people with mental disabilities. It would be a great fit. We decided to go for it.

My biggest challenge was still convincing my mother—not only that it was time for me to go, but that I would, in fact, be safe. It took a few days. But when I saw her put a box of cornflakes in a cardboard box with "Food for Cam's Apartment" written in felt marker, I knew we were on the same page.

• • •

It was mid-November, and I was on my knees in the bathtub with the shower pounding cold water all over my body. And it felt wonderful.

Not that I wasn't freezing. But I was freezing by myself. And that had never happened before. All my life, someone had bathed me or scrubbed me down in the shower, and now I was alone, showering myself in my own bathroom of my own apartment.

Getting there required an act of faith. But I'd been waiting all night—hell, I'd been waiting for years. The night before, as I climbed into bed for the first time in my new home, I'd set the alarm fifteen minutes earlier than usual just to make sure I'd have enough time, and mentally rehearsed the moves I'd be making, over and over again. First time getting into a tub on your own, Tait. Screw it up and you could wind up face down in the tub until Jerry has to go to the can.

I pulled myself to my feet and hung on to a grab bar on the side of the tub. Next, I leaned over and latched on to the grab bar just below the soap dish attached to the wall. Taking a deep breath, I swung my left leg over the side of the bathtub, and then brought the other leg over and gently knelt down on both knees, facing the taps.

I turned on the taps—and discovered the flaw in the plan. The apartment we'd moved into had never been lived in, and someone had neglected to turn on the hot water tank. It didn't faze me a bit. I was just so damn happy that I didn't even feel the cold, and just as excited when I navigated safely back into my chair when I was done.

Okay, Tait, you're eighteen and you can get in and out of the shower. Now, let's see what else you can do.

In a sense, the shower success was a trigger. When I moved in with Jerry, I wanted to view him more as a roommate than a personal assistant. I found ways to do more for myself, like getting my undershorts, placing them carefully on the floor, putting my feet in the right spots and then pulling them up to my thighs before standing up for the rest. I had never challenged myself to do it before, and it meant Jerry didn't have to do everything for me. It was surprising how much that did for my sense of dignity.

It may be difficult to understand, but the thing I began to treasure about my newly independent living was the sense of normalcy, the comfort that came with establishment of a routine. With Jerry working at the group home, I would go home for weekends. Mom and Dad would drop me off at the apartment Sunday nights, I'd wait for Jerry to come home, we'd visit, compare weekend notes and plan our week. Looking back, the break was a good thing and kept our relationship fresh.

Weekday mornings, Jerry would drive me to NAIT because he said it was the right thing to do. Personally, I think it was because I managed to get him a handicapped parking spot right outside the door; Jerry always liked good parking. I would get my own way home and then we would have dinner together. Ah, domesticity!

Jerry and I got along quite well and never really had a big fight. I did hear him swear under his breath one morning when he found the pair of dress pants he had ironed so carefully the night before and hung over a kitchen chair now crumpled on the kitchen floor. I'd gotten up in the middle of the night for a drink of water. My front wheel somehow caught the pants and dragged them to the floor and I couldn't pick them up.

The only other misunderstanding came one night when he brought home a dinner guest, a young lady whom I knew from our church. I didn't realize he was trying to make an impression on her, although I should have. After dinner, I stuck around to visit and started calling some of our mutual friends and asking them over. The more the merrier, I thought. It kind of ruined Jerry's evening. He was just getting the fire crackling, he'd poured some wine and put on some mood music—and the doorbell started ringing. He later told me, very clearly, what he thought of me turning his night of romance into an impromptu drop-in party.

Jerry was doing a great job with helping me, and I wanted to give him a little more freedom. We had a two-bedroom townhouse with a full basement. Having two roommates, I thought, might provide a little more flexibility for everyone. In came Ken Steller, another friend from NAIT, a quiet guy but a brilliant writer. Good thing, too. A few weeks after Ken moved in, Jerry accepted a job with a video company in Fort McMurray.

It's never easy to say goodbye to a friend, and he'd been a great one. But he'd helped me prove that I could live independently, and not just to the skeptics. I'd proved it to myself.

15

What Would Your Dog Like on His Pizza?

Gary Chomyn was a huge support in making me a part of the RTA family. He noticed a space in the radio production studio and asked if I would like to move my typewriter and desk into the studio so I could have more interaction with everyone. I jumped at the chance. But he was doing even more, which I didn't know about.

Since I was deemed a "special student," Eric Candy didn't think it was necessary to have the commercials I was writing produced to be aired on the NAIT radio station. Gary went to bat for me, saying the quality of my work was worthy of being produced— and I was a student in technology.

And that lit another fire.

I telephoned Daryl Hooke at CHED Radio, who had told me to call him if I ever got to NAIT.

"Hi. Remember me?" I asked.

"No, I'm sorry, I don't," Daryl said. At least he was honest.

I reminded him about calling and what he'd said.

"So," I said brightly, "here I am."

Daryl came to NAIT the next week and we had lunch. He read some of my writing and said it was fairly good, which was great encouragement. A few weeks later, he mailed me some sheets of CHED copy paper with a few fact sheets from Shakey's Pizza, a familiar spot for our family. I wanted to refresh my mind about Shakey's, so I had Dad take me for pizza and beer. Hey, it was research. The next day I wrote a commercial about Shakey's being such a great family restaurant that there was even room for family dogs—well, not really, but it made good copy—and mailed it to Daryl. A day or so later, he called me in the radio production studio at NAIT with some news.

"I can't tell you why," he said. "But you might want to listen to CHED tonight between ten and eleven."

Our family gathered around the old green kitchen radio that night. Sure enough, about ten minutes after ten, my Shakey's spot was on the air.

Mom gave me a hug and kissed my forehead. "This could be your start in the media," she said.

• • •

I was learning the basics of how radio production worked, but I was learning a much more valuable lesson—how to interact with people without disabilities. I'd had such great experiences with so many people when I was a kid. Now, as a young adult, I had to teach myself how to be with people my own age. Again, my dear friend Gary Chomyn came through for me.

I had always wanted to laugh about my disability with others. But my parents—especially Mom—really discouraged it. So did people around Glenrose. Gary and I were chatting one day when I told him my father thought he would become a very rich man because of my disability.

Gary frowned at me and asked me what the hell I was talking about.

"Oh, yeah," I said. "When the doctor made his final diagnosis and said, 'Mr. Tait, your son has CP,' Dad ran all the way to the bank. He thought he meant stock in Canadian Pacific."

Gary howled, and repeated the story to friends all day. For those I had not yet gotten to know, it didn't just give them a chuckle, it let them see me in a more positive light.

Gary started making jokes about me, too. Some people thought it was cruel, but to me it was a great form of being accepted. And when others saw Gary and I joking around, it made them more comfortable around me.

Leaving a party at Gary's one night, he got my shoes and started to help me put them on. "We're going to dress you up funny," he said. And then he put them on the wrong feet. I got in the cab and I don't know who was laughing more, Gary or me.

Before long, I was daring to get into the spirit of things myself. One afternoon I put classmate Sandy Pywell in my chair, pulled myself up behind it, and pushed him down the hallway, Sandy mimicking my speech and waving his arms all over the place. It got us some dirty looks, but Sandy and I laughed like hell, and so did the rest of our class, who knew by now that key difference between laughing with and laughing at.

Humour was helping break down so many barriers at NAIT. It really helps to start off your day looking for something funny. It's an inheritance from my dad. Humour has been my constant companion, and has opened many doors. I am especially grateful to Gary for showing me that it was okay to be funny, and I appreciate the people around me at NAIT who laughed along with us. It was a great confidence boost.

In time, I got more comfortable writing radio spots and really enjoyed working with sound effects and music. I credit my parents' musical talents for giving me a good sense of timing, and

I loved working with producers, making suggestions on where and when music was used in my spots. There was a magical feeling when I wheeled by the radio studio and heard one of my spots being aired.

I was having a terrific time at NAIT in so many ways. Then, in early November 1977, Candy called me into his office to ask an interesting question. My broadcast writing course was coming to an end at the end of the month, and so was my time writing radio copy. Candy said he originally had thought I would stay at NAIT for only three months, or a quarter term. But a television instructor, John McClay, who was also a big supporter of what I was trying to do, suggested I take television pre-production starting in December under my special student status. Then, the following March, I could take the television production course, which ended in May.

I was speechless. My high school scholarship covered my NAIT tuition for an entire year. It would be perfect. Then Candy said something that brought tears to my eyes: "We all love having you here, Cam. And we don't want to see you go."

The television pre-production class was wonderful, with just ten of us in the writing office. Not only was it a very creative environment, my fellow students were very helpful to me.

I began to learn that anything can be done with a little adaptation and creativity. Everyone in TV pre-production needed five copies of everything they wrote, since there were more people involved in producing a commercial for television. I had trouble getting carbon paper in my typewriter, so John McClay talked to someone in the NAIT business office and I was allowed to take my script to the office and make copies on the Xerox machine.

At last came my dream to write broadcast news. We produced a newscast every Friday and each of us rewrote wire copy to make it a little more of a personal situation. I really started enjoying writing news, and since I couldn't read it on air, I was given extra copy to write.

We wrote television commercials and had to produce a 30-minute special. My buddy Gary was in television pre-production with me and I asked him to interview my mentor, Eddie Keen from CHED Radio. Gary said he would but I had to write the questions. I called Eddie and arranged a date for him to come to NAIT. The interview was very timely, since the *Edmonton Sun* was just starting publication in town. Being a veteran newspaperman, Eddie had several thoughts about Edmonton becoming a city with two newspapers.

16

"I'm Pretty Proud of You"

In March 1978, the phone rang in our apartment well after 10:30 p.m., causing us to think something was wrong. It was Marv Sather from the Kiwanis Club, telling me that I was one of five finalists in the Salute to Youth program in Edmonton.

"We need you at the Westin Hotel tomorrow night for the banquet and the award ceremony," he said. "But can you come early for pictures?"

I assured him I'd be there, hung up, and called Mom and Dad.

"I kind of knew it would be you calling," Dad said. "I guess you heard the news."

He'd provided information on me for my nominator, he said, but wouldn't tell me who it was, only that it hadn't been him.

The keynote speaker at the dinner was Dick Irvin of *Hockey Night in Canada*. Salute to Youth recognized students in the Edmonton area who had achieved a few good things, either in their schooling or community activities. The five winners and their families met in a small banquet room off the main ballroom. *Journal* reporter Alan Chambers interviewed all of us, and asked me about my writing.

"You should think about writing for newspaper," Alan said. (Seven years later, Alan was my city editor for a few months at the *Journal*.)

We had dinner with the winners and their families before the award ceremony. During conversation with a few of the Kinsmen members, I casually mentioned how I loved watching Dick Irvin on Hockey Night in Canada and how honoured I would be to meet him. One of the members smiled widely but did not say a word.

My old pal Randy Kilburn from 630 CHED popped into the banquet room to say hello and reminded me how I used to phone him every night when I was in Grade 11. "But you don't have to phone me tonight," he said with a chuckle. "I came to get the story myself."

After we ate, the other four winners and I were taken to the kitchen and then were introduced by another one of my role models, Eddie Keen from CHED.

"Let's introduce Cam last," one of the organizers said.

I peeked out into the main ballroom and couldn't believe my eyes. It was packed with eight hundred people. The dinner was a major fundraiser for the Kinsmen.

Eddie Keen introduced me and talked about the two books I had written in school. He also mentioned my time at NAIT and how I wanted to become a writer. He said I had a great attitude and spirit—something I had never heard before, but I was very humbled by it.

The crowd rose to their feet as I was wheeled to the head table and presented with my award. I looked over to the far wall of the banquet room and saw Mom and Dad standing with the other parents. It was great to share the moment with them.

Al McCann, who worked for CFRN Television sports for years, was emcee.

"Cam, there is someone here who wants to meet you," Al said. I saw Dick Irvin walking toward me.

"Dick Irvin, meet Mr. Cam Tait."

We shook hands in front of the crowd. I was thrilled.

Mom and Dad drove me home. Dad took me into my apartment and helped me off with my jacket. I asked him again who had nominated me. This time he gave in. "It was Eddie Keen," he said. He went to the door, opened it, but then stopped.

"You need to know I am pretty proud of you tonight," he said. It was a special moment. I had always known the love was there, and the pride at how I'd faced my situation. But that was the only time he ever said the words. It was the perfect ending for an unforgettable night.

● ● ●

I was flying so high it's a wonder my chair didn't sprout wings. Everything I tried seemed to work out; every break I needed, I got.

Take hockey, which has always been such a big part of my life. The Edmonton Crusaders were a Junior A team playing in the Alberta Junior Hockey League. The owner was a businessman, Rod Matthews, who had a son who played with my brother, Brad. I asked Matthews if I could write stories for the Crusader program and he said I could.

But he didn't stop there. He arranged for me to ride the team bus for trips to Calgary and Red Deer. When I got to the rink, three or four guys helped me out of my chair and assisted me walking onto the bus. The same thing happened, in reverse, when we got home. We had an old bus from the mid-1950s and the heater often didn't work on cold nights coming back to Edmonton. I never felt the cold, though. To be part of the team was precious to me.

Some guys got it and some guys ain't. I wasn't best man at friend Kevin Shaigec's wedding in 1993, but I clearly had a good time.

I knew a few of the guys from midget AAA teams that I had followed a few years earlier, especially Kevin Shaigec. Kevin took me under his wing and introduced me to several of the guys on the team. He invited me to team parties and we had our fair share of fun. The hours, of course, were crazy, as they are for all junior hockey clubs, who bounce along on buses while they dream of the NHL, with its big money and charter planes. It was usually two or three in the morning by the time one of the equipment managers got me home, and I had to be up by 7:30 to get to class.

Mom and a few others thought I should stay home from class when we got in so late from the road, but that would be the easy way out. Everyone else on the team had to get up and go to class, so why shouldn't I? I mean, I had an advantage from the rest of the guys on the team: I didn't have to play, and I sat in the stands watching the game from my wheelchair. Seriously, though, I think the schedule of being with a junior hockey club helped me form a good work ethic.

Near the end of the regular season, we played a road game against the Red Deer Rustlers. On the way down, I got in a poker game and luck was on my side. I won eighteen dollars by the time we hit the Red Deer city limits. We beat the Rustlers that night, which made a happier bus ride home. After I staggered to my seat in the second row, I asked to join the poker game on the way home.

"Are you kidding?" asked forward George Orlecki. "You won all our money on the way down. Fuck off, Cam."

I was beyond ecstatic. That was the first time anyone told me to F-off, which told me I was no longer the guy in the wheelchair who liked hockey; I was now one of the boys—a wonderful feeling of acceptance. And no matter how cold it was on the ride home, I didn't feel it at all. Being accepted was a very comfortable feeling.

Oh, yeah, I was on a roll.

I invited a lovely redhead named Jan Currey to one of our home games and she sat with me in our team booth above the south goal at Jasper Place Arena. Jan came to the majority of the rest of our regular season games before we entered a very exciting first round of playoffs against the Fort Saskatchewan Traders.

The dress code of junior hockey has always been intriguing to me. Not only were the guys, including me, dressed well in suits and ties, the players' girlfriends wore dresses to the games. Jan and I were not dating as such, but we were hanging around the guys and their girlfriends, and she had met a few of the women the other players were dating.

When we had our first home playoff game against the Traders, Jan showed up looking great in dress clothes and decided to sit with the other girls for the game while I sat in the booth with some of our injured guys. Again, I felt a tremendous pride in being accepted—and had a wonderful young lady waiting for me after the game, just like the other guys.

Mom and Dad came with Jan and me to our year-end banquet. After the dinner, the team presented me with a jersey with my name on the back. It is one of the most treasured gifts I have ever received.

Being a small part of the Edmonton Crusaders made a huge impact on my confidence and self-worth. And why not? Things really couldn't get much better: I was in a course that I loved, had moved out on my own, was part of a Junior A hockey team and had countless new friends.

And then my world imploded.

• • •

With one week left in my course at NAIT, Eric Candy asked me into his office late one afternoon and shut the door before he sat down. Maybe I was naïve, or banking on my incredible luck to continue. I really thought he was going to tell me he had a broadcast writing job for me.

Candy sat down and laid his glasses on his desk. He took a deep breath.

"Cam, you know your time here at NAIT is coming to an end," he began. "We have enjoyed having you here. But you're not a great writer. You're mediocre, at best. Your chances of finding work are very slim. In fact, I do not think any media outlet will hire you. They don't hire people in wheelchairs to be writers.

"I know that's your dream. But I really would not be doing my job if I did not tell you that. And the sooner you realize it, the better off you will be."

I was absolutely stunned. I'd felt I was on my way to fulfilling my biggest dream, and now it was collapsing like a punctured balloon. I could barely wheel out of his office. Slowly, I wheeled down the hallway, which had always been filled with laughter, enthusiasm and endless opportunities. It was one of the loneliest minutes of my life.

I couldn't tell anyone. If I did, I would be giving in to Candy's thinking. I wasn't about to go down that road... yet. It was utterly devastating. From the moment I met him, he had always been so encouraging, so kind, so accommodating. For him to do an about-face and be so discouraging just did not make any sense.

And the fates weren't through with me yet. Remember my

joy at being able to take a hot shower by myself? Well, as I got ready to leave NAIT, my mental tail between my legs, I went in to shower again as I had every day since.

By now I had the routine down: grip the grab bar, stand up, get both feet into the tub. But as I was slowly dropping to my knees, I slipped and fell. The water wasn't yet turned on. I always did that once I was sitting on my haunches. This time, I landed on my back—not hard—with my head just below the water tap. No problem. I knew all I had to do was turn on my right side, get my left arm underneath me, and then get on my hands and knees. Easy enough, which is why I didn't call for help.

But as I turned, my head hit the hot water lever, and turned it on full blast. My left shoulder was touching the spout where the scalding water was pouring out. The pain was incredible.

I screamed, loudly and repeatedly. It seemed like forever before Ken, who'd been sleeping in the basement, stormed into the bathroom, took one quick glance at the situation and turned off the tap.

"I'm okay," I said as I gathered myself and looked at my shoulder. At that very moment, a layer of burnt skin fell into the bathtub.

"I think we need to get you to the hospital," Ken said. He was right. I had third-degree burns and still bear the scar. I often think of when we moved in back in November, when the hot water tank wasn't turned on. Perhaps we should have kept it in the off position.

Mom wanted me to move home after I ended up in hot water. I told her I had no such plans, and that accidents happen—no matter where I lived. She didn't really buy it, so we came to a compromise. I would never have a shower again without someone in the house.

I sat back to take stock: leaving school, no job to go to and assurances from a teacher for whom I had such great respect that I wasn't likely to get one, and a shoulder burned when I was attacked by my own bathtub.

I was on a roll, all right. Downhill. So much for school days.

17
····

Rimmer

His name was Paul Rimstead. He was my friend and my mentor and the guy who, more than anyone else, shoved me into the newspaper business. He also happened to be one of the finest newspaper columnists this country has ever produced, and to say his approach was a little off the wall would be like saying Howard Hughes was a teensy bit eccentric.

Examples? Where to begin?

In 1968, "Rimmer" went to a horse sale and fell in love with a spavined three-year-old filly named Annabelle. Don't ask me why. Her four-race career to that point had earned her $200 for one show finish. Her ears stood out at 45-degree angles, and as she was paraded around the ring she looked like they'd forgotten to hitch her to the milk wagon. But who can explain love? Rimmer and two of his Toronto Telegram buddies ponied up the $1,100 asking price. There is a chance that alcohol was involved.

Deciding that Annabelle needed some recognition, Rimmer added "the Wonder Horse" to her name, set up a series of public appearances at which his Dixieland band (Rimmer was the drummer) would follow in her wake, and hired wrestler Sweet

Daddy Siki to be her bodyguard lest the paparazzi become too persistent. Then he called a press conference at the swish Royal York Hotel to announce that Annabelle would be entered in the Kentucky Derby and to defray expenses, five thousand shares would be available at a buck a pop. Oh, and yes, Annabelle would be at the press conference.

Naturally, Annabelle's exploits were covered daily in Rimmer's wildly popular column, and such was its appeal that Annabelle's press conference drew a crowd of several hundred, including half of the Toronto city council. Maybe it was the promise of free mint juleps "direct from Kentucky." The mint actually came from Cleveland, but Rimmer clocked the consumption and marvelled in the next day's column that the crowd knocked back three hundred in the first half hour.

And yes, as promised, Annabelle did appear, riding up the freight elevator and striding down the Royal York hallway to the Manitoba Room on an old carpet thoughtfully laid out by a hotel staffer with a rose in his lapel. She was on her best behaviour, holding still under the hot camera lights and submitting to microphones stuck in her face in hope of eliciting a snort. But the conference dragged on, and finally she protested the only way a genteel lady could, all over the Manitoba coat of arms.

No, she never did make it to Kentucky. In Rimmer's defence, the press conference was held on April 1.

Lest I forget—the Dixieland band also came into play a year or so later when he marched it into a breakfast meeting of the Football Reporters of Canada during Grey Cup week, led by a well-endowed topless stripper holding Rimmer's drums waist-high, Rimmer's arms around her so he could keep the beat. Periodically he would pound the drum, then reach up and tap her breasts. As the music stopped, he yelled, "Let's hear it for my drums!" and got a standing ovation. And in the year post-Annabelle he entered the world Monopoly championships in Detroit after billing himself as the Canadian champion, although he hadn't played for years and was crushed to find out there was no longer a milk bottle token. He arrived in full tuxedo and top hat and actually made it past the first round. If only he'd had the milk bottle...

Rimmer came into my life right about the time I figured all the doors to meaningful media employment were shut. Ken Sellar had taken a job at a Saskatoon TV station, so I was living at home again. I had nothing to show for numerous job applications but a pile of rejection letters.

It was a no-win situation. I needed to work in a major centre because the small centres didn't have the accessible apartments and personal care support I needed, but the radio stations in those centres wanted people with experience, which I didn't have and couldn't get without starting in a small centre, which didn't have the services—accessible housing and transportation—for people with disabilities to live independently.

Discouragement was killing my motivation. Why send out another resume when all it would bring was another rejection? It took my mother to get that out of my system, which she did in typical Mom fashion. She dropped a bomb on my self-pity and blew it to smithereens.

Her suggestion that I go back to school and take a journalism course was rejected out of hand. Newspaper reporting never really interested me. I read the sports section faithfully, but the urge to be a reporter was lukewarm at best. So, one day at the crack of noon—because that's when your day starts when you're not working—as she was having lunch while I dug into breakfast, she handed me a copy of a monthly paper called *The Spokesman*, which dealt with issues for people with disabilities.

"They're looking for volunteer writers," she said. "You should call them."

"Not interested," I said. "I don't have time to volunteer."

Suddenly, the room turned cold.

"Is that right?" she said. "Let me ask you, where would you be right now if our friends didn't volunteer when we were doing patterning? What if they were too busy to come help you?"

The answer absolutely scared the hell out of me. In fact, if it had not been for our volunteers—the lifeblood of the patterning program—I would not be sitting up at the kitchen table, feeding myself.

"Could you hand me the phone, please?" I asked sheepishly. "I need to call *The Spokesman.*"

The Spokesman editor, Larry Pempeit, himself a quadriplegic who worked out of a wheelchair, told me I could start writing a volunteer sports column, once a month. Just like that, I was in the newspaper business, sort of. And maybe there is something to that karma stuff, because one week later, I met Rimmer.

Paul came to Edmonton in the late 1970s when the *Edmonton Sun* took a run at the *Journal*. His column was still a feature of the *Toronto Sun,* but the chain had him filing a lot of them from Edmonton to give our paper in the chain a boost. His unique style was an instant hit as he drew readers into his oddball world with tales of his jazz band, his excessive drinking, his afraid-I-might-live hangovers and, most importantly, his adventures meeting ordinary people, the sort with whom any reader could identify. That first night, over drinks at the Point After sports bar, he gave me a crash course in journalism.

"The most important thing you'll ever write," Paul told me, lighting a cigarette, "is what people say. Quotes. That's the most important point of a story."

I took it all in from a man who had been around for decades, covering the Toronto Maple Leafs, big boxing events and so much more. He showed me how to make every sentence a paragraph and scribbled notes on a bar napkin for me to take home.

I felt a new energy from meeting Paul. Still, I felt there was something missing. I was writing the monthly column for *The*

Spokesman, but I didn't have a job. Paul said he understood. And he had an idea.

"I want you to write every day, five hundred words," Paul said. This was 1979. No faxes. No email.

"When you're done, call me and I will call a cab to come bring it to me," he said. "I will read it, and then call you with what I think. But do me a favour—write every day. Write about whatever you want, and write about what you do. But write."

In the years to come, Paul kept his word, and more. Whenever he was in Edmonton, he'd call the day I had a story in the *Journal* and give me encouragement and advice. I was taken by his kindness, especially since he was writing for the *Sun.*

I read Paul's columns faithfully, studying his style and rhythm. As I learned throughout my career, writing humour on a regular basis is very difficult. But he managed to do it six days a week and did it amazingly well.

Paul's storytelling talent is something I will never forget. His deadline was 7:00 p.m. Edmonton time. One afternoon I met him for a drink in the lobby bar of the Westin Hotel. A drink? Not around Paul.

I have always been early for everything—hell, I want to be early for my funeral. So at 6:00 p.m., I started looking at my watch, thinking he would be getting up to his room to write a column.

"Let's have another drink," he said, motioning the waitress. And we did. Paul was in no hurry.

Finally, at 6:35, Paul shoved a crumpled bar napkin with a few scribbled notes into his shirt pocket. He took a final sip of his double Scotch. "Okay, let's go," he said.

I had asked Paul earlier if I could watch him write. We entered his room and I thought he'd haul out his portable typewriter and pound it like a maniac. Wrong. Paul went to his mini-bar, sat down at the desk, and dialed the phone.

"Collect from Rimstead," he growled as someone from the *Toronto Sun* answered, then dug out his bar napkin and spread it on the desk. That was all he had in front of him. And then he started dictating—spelling words, giving punctuation and paragraph breaks. I just soaked it all in. But he saved the best for last.

I looked at the clock radio beside his bed. It read 6:59. Paul paused for a second and took a sip of his Scotch.

"Can you give me a word count? I think I'm almost there," he said, aiming for his 750-word column.

"Seven-hundred and forty-eight, eh? Kind of thought so."

He added a final paragraph and then said that magic number reporters used to write at the end of their piece.

"Thirty" was a throwback to the old days, when linotypes produced the stories in lead slugs measured in "ems" that were bolted into the page before it was shipped to the presses. To indicate the end of a story on the page there'd be a single lead line—a long hyphen, if you will—thirty ems wide. When reporters finished typing their stories, they wrote "30" to tell the desk man (and later the guy setting it on the linotype) that they'd reached the end.

Paul hung up and poured himself a drink. "I'm done work for the day. I deserve this," he said.

I was absolutely amazed when I read Paul's column in the newspaper the next day. It looked and read like he'd spent hours over a typewriter, mulling over every word he wrote.

But Paul was more than just a teacher. He often asked me to be his "date" for sportsmen's dinners in Edmonton, introducing me to Oilers' and Eskimos' players and executives. He also encouraged me to keep laughing with my disability. We were just getting started with our dessert at one dinner when he asked me if I liked the blue-grey suit he was wearing.

"I am wearing it in your honour, you know," he said. "I called the hotel earlier today and they told me they were having cherries jubilee for dessert. So I wore my grey suit because I knew you might be flinging cherries around—and they would blend into my suit."

Nobody else at the table laughed. Paul and I howled.

I swear, whatever oddball gene Rimmer had must have been catching. In July that year I talked him into doing something that even he thought was over the weirdness border.

"I'll do it," he said finally. "But if you spill any of my double Scotch, you're buying me a new one."

I extended my hand. "We have a deal," I said. Then, in front of a jam-packed crowd in the Crown Suite on the Westin Hotel's top floor, I pulled myself out of my wheelchair, grabbed the handles to stand up, got my balance, and looked him in the eye.

"Get in," I ordered.

Paul got up from his chair and plunked himself in my wheelchair. "Just don't spill my drink," he said, cradling the glass.

By then, people—including a blonde-haired young kid named Gretzky who was making one of his first public appearances in Edmonton—looked up and started laughing as Paul gently directed me out of the suite door to the elevator.

"Why are we going down to the bar when we have all the free booze in the world in the suite?" I asked.

"Because we can!" Paul barked. "Now, be careful and don't spill my drink."

We got in the elevator and Paul pushed the button. We arrived in the lobby with no problem. When we got there, of course, there were curious looks from guests checking in, bellmen and cab drivers standing at the door.

"Don't spill my drink, now," he kept saying, louder and louder, playing to the gathering crowd. "Okay, let's go over and sit by George" (as in George Ward, whose name I'd seen on the front page of the *Journal*, but whom I'd never met). It must have been a grand entrance we made, me pushing newspaper legend Paul Rimstead in my wheelchair.

"Can we join you?" Paul asked George, who was sitting by himself at a corner table. George agreed, and my life changed forever.

After we got comfortable—Paul in an easy chair and me back in my wheelchair—we started chatting. Rimmer told George about my current job, and my dream to write.

"You wanna write for me?" George asked in his gruff, yet friendly Prince Edward Island voice. I swallowed hard, refusing to believe my ears.

"Are you serious?" I asked.

"Yes. Send me some stuff and we'll see how you do." George said. Then he leaned forward to emphasize his point. "I'm going to be honest with you. If it's a piece of crap, into the garbage it goes."

It was a message he repeated about every three minutes over the next hour or so. There'd be no free pass because of my disability. I appreciated that so much. It was all I'd ever asked. We talked about when I would write and what I could cover. I wouldn't be on staff. I'd be freelancing. I was so excited I could barely speak, but I couldn't wait to tell my folks, so Paul took me up to his room to make the call. As I hung up, Paul sat down on the bed and put his hands on my shoulders.

"Cammie, this is a great break, so work hard," he said. "And don't screw it up."

Now, it might be obvious that Paul liked to drink. Yes, he did. It didn't happen very often, but there were a few times when he drank too much to file a column. The *Sun* had a nice paragraph ready to place beside Paul's picture should the occasion arise: "Mr. Rimstead is unavailable today. He will be back tomorrow." Many people, though, knew the real reason when he wasn't in the paper.

His drinking finally caught up with him. Paul spent his forty-fifth birthday in early 1980 in the Royal Alexandra Hospital in Edmonton. He was very ill and doctors frankly told him if he continued drinking he would die. So he stopped for a while, but eventually started again.

Paul's visits to Edmonton became less frequent since the local *Sun* developed its own identity and columnists in the early 1980s. When he did hit town, we had lots of laughs. One night he introduced me to his good friend, former Toronto Maple Leaf forward Eddie Shack, who couldn't read or write. "This is my lucky day," Paul crowed. "I get to spend it with one guy who can't read or write and another one who can't talk."

Paul's last visit to Edmonton was in 1982, but we kept in touch over the telephone. The last time I talked to him was in 1986 when he was at his cabin in Bass Lake, Ontario.

"Wait a second while I get my drink," he said as he put the phone down.

"You're drinking?" I asked. "What are you drinking?"

"Rye and Coke," he replied.

I knew Paul hated rye. And he once told me he would never mix alcohol with pop. Why was he drinking it now?

"Doctor said I need to cut down my drinking," he explained. "I hate rye and Coke. So I figure it will make me drink less."

On the evening of May 24, 1987, I had just filed a story in the *Journal* offices. A copy editor from the news desk walked over to my desk with a story he had ripped off the printer from the news wire.

"I thought you might like to know about this," he said. It was a Canadian Press story from Fort Lauderdale, Florida, on Paul's death at age 52. I knew his lifestyle would eventually catch up with him. But I didn't think it would be that soon.

I looked up from reading the story and saw the environment I was in—reporters on telephones, others at computer terminals writing stories, copy editors carefully inspecting hundreds of words before sending them to be printed on a page. I was right where I wanted to be. I knew I wouldn't have been sitting there without Paul Rimstead's support. And I felt him smiling down on me.

18
····

Terry Who?

Pour enough drinks and any reporter or columnist who isn't a flat-out liar will admit to the big one that got away, the story he should have had but screwed up or couldn't see when it was right there in front of him. Cold sober, this is mine...

A few months before I started freelancing with the *Journal*, Gary McPherson phoned me at home to introduce himself. Gary was the general manager of the Alberta Northern Lights wheelchair basketball team, had read a few of my sports columns in *The Spokesman* and suggested that I start covering his team. I soon found out that wheelchair basketball was only one of Gary's many tools as he battled for recognition and support for the disabled community. Given his own circumstances, his commitment and dedication were truly amazing.

In 1965, as his family was vacationing in Edmonton from their home in the Yukon, nine-year-old Gary was one of the thousands of children caught by the polio epidemic that swept over North America. It left him paralyzed almost from head to toe and confined to an iron lung. Doctors doubted he'd survive. Clearly, they didn't know Gary.

Hard work and sheer determination freed him from the iron lung, but he still needed a ventilator to breathe. So, he set to work to master a technique known as "frog breathing" to wean himself off the respirator during the day. For Gary, that was simply the step that allowed him to get out into the community and get to work.

Gary refused to let his physical limitations stop him. He could move his left hand enough to click a computer mouse. The advent of the electric wheelchair widened his horizons, but even before that, he was office manager for future premier Don Getty and later chaired the premier's Council on the Status of Persons with Disabilities. He honed his public speaking skills. He was an active member of the Junior Chamber of Commerce, and an adjunct professor in the University of Alberta's school of physical activity, and later found time to write his autobiography, *With Every Breath I Take.*

I'd never followed basketball, but I read up on it so I wouldn't make a fool of myself when the Northern Lights began tryouts. George Ward said the *Journal* would be interested in some wheelchair basketball stories, not so much games as human-interest material. And I had a dandy, or could have, if I'd listened to Gary.

As part of his plan to showcase the sport, Gary had set up an eight-team post-Christmas tournament in 1979. Because he wanted the Northern Lights to make a good showing locally and thereby trigger interest, he'd bolstered his tournament roster with five players from the archrival Vancouver Cable Cars. As they practised, he called to me.

"Hey, Tait," he began. "I got a scoop for you. See that guy on the beanbag chair—the guy with the curly brown hair?"

I nodded, but wasn't really paying attention. I was too busy making notes on another player I was writing about.

"He has cancer. Lost a leg, and that's why he's playing wheelchair basketball. He's going to run across Canada in the spring."

"Uh-huh," I muttered, still making notes.

"He's kind of a shy guy and hasn't had anything written about him. He's right over there—go talk to him."

Well, I knew a good news story when I heard one. Hadn't I been in the newspaper business for four months?

"Thanks Gary, but I don't have time today," I said, tucking my notepad and tape recorder into my briefcase. "And I don't think it will ever amount to anything much."

And then I left, without talking to the kid from Vancouver. The kid named Terry Fox.

I look back on that day now and don't know whether to laugh or cry. Because I didn't just miss out on the chance to write what would have been the first major story on Terry Fox and what would become the legendary Marathon of Hope. There was another of the Cable Car imports sitting there with him—the guy who'd talked Fox into taking up wheelchair basketball in an effort to pull him out of the emotional funk brought on by the loss of his leg. Give me a minute and I'll think of his name…

Oh, yeah, Rick Hansen. Didn't write about him, either. When you're hot, you're hot.

In my defence, Rick hadn't yet mentioned his own dream to go around the world by wheelchair, the dream that would become the Man in Motion World Tour, starting in 1985 to tie in with Vancouver's Expo 86. He told me about it over breakfast at a tournament in San Jose in early 1983, when I had resumed covering the Northern Lights for both *The Spokesman* and the *Journal* and travelled with them along the US west coast. I did write about the MIM Tour then, as well as many other Hansen stories later as he became a world-class wheelchair marathoner, and the first person with a disability to take physical education at the University of British Columbia. But the Christmas 1979 double strikeout still haunted me.

Fast forward to March 1985. The Northern Lights were

heading home on a chartered bus after a big tournament win. We hit Tumwater, Washington, and heard that the Man in Motion tour, now in its third day, was stopped there overnight. Well, of course we had to get the name of the motel and detour the bus to see their old basketball buddy. It was only neighbourly.

Our driver parked the bus right in front of Rick's door, then got out to knock. As soon as he vacated the driver's seat, one of the players climbed in and hit the horn for about twenty seconds to announce our arrival. Okay, it was 10:30 p.m., the tour group was exhausted and sound asleep, but what are friends for?

Rick gamely wheeled out to the bus for a visit, and he gave me a five-minute interview, which I turned into a feature story when I returned to Edmonton.

I wrote two more stories about the tour via telephone interviews—one when Rick was in Australia, and the other from Poland. But the tour was now attracting nation-wide attention. To give it the coverage it had now earned, you'd have to have someone there. I desperately wanted that someone to be me.

In June 1986, I submitted a proposal to the *Journal* to cover Rick when he came back to Canada that August. The first answer was no. The paper would cover the border crossing with wire stories from Newfoundland. But, two weeks later, the *Journal* city editor, Wendy Koenig, said they'd reconsidered, and I was going to meet Rick in St. John's, Newfoundland. My travelling partner was *Journal* chief photographer Jim Cochrane, who helped me out with things like dressing.

We got into St. John's well after midnight. It was still hot. The air-conditioning system in the hotel was not working and the airline had lost our luggage. By 3:00 a.m., I asked myself just whose bright idea this insane road trip had been. Oh, yeah. Mine.

We met Rick's media manager, Muriel Honey, in the hotel lobby after breakfast. Muriel and I had spoken over the telephone

Covering the Man in Motion tour stop in Newfoundland made a great photo op with Amanda Reid, Journal *photographer Jim Cochrane and tour members Don Alder and Nancy Thompson. The guy next to me you probably know.* PHOTO BY *JIM TAYLOR*

many times and I asked her if Rick knew I was in town. She said no, but she would tell him.

"No, please don't do that," I asked. "Let's surprise him."

Jim and I drove to the most easterly point of North America, Cape Spear. It was beautiful, even though the weather had dramatically shifted into cool. Jim had instructions from the newsroom to get a picture of Rick and me for the paper the next day. He wheeled my chair next to the ramp that Rick would push up to reach the stage, just a few hundred feet west of the Atlantic Ocean.

I was amazed at the organization and excitement of the event. We waited ten minutes before Rick and the official party arrived. When they did, there were television and newspaper cameras on Rick. At first I felt a great need to join the scrum in case I missed the quote of the decade. But then I decided to sit back, enjoy the show, and let Rick come to me.

And that's exactly what happened. The cameras followed Rick as he turned the corner up the ramp. When he saw me, he offered a warm handshake and put his hand on my elbow.

"Hey, what are you doing here? How are the boys in Edmonton?" he asked.

"We're hanging in there," I replied.

"How long are you in Newfoundland with us?" he asked.

I told him we were there for five days. Rick said when the tour slowed down outside of St. John's, we would have a visit. Then he wheeled up the ramp to the podium.

Jim slapped me on the back and let out his infectious laugh. "I got my picture. So I guess we're not fired."

"Maybe you're not. But I still have a story to write," I said.

After speeches, Rick hit the highway and wheeled up a steep hill right out of St. John's. Jim and I jumped into the car and went up the hill and a few hundred yards farther. Then we waited for the motorcade—a police car, Rick, his van and a few support vehicles—to wheel by. We did this a few times and then I got the ride of a lifetime.

Jim helped me out of the car and told me to hang on. Then, four days before his fiftieth birthday, he tipped me back in my chair and started pushing me down the highway beside Rick. I was amazed at the speed he was achieving. Jim was out of breath but we kept pace for half a mile. That was the only time I wheeled beside Rick.

An hour later, I was sitting on the roadside again, waiting for the motorcade next to a boy about 10 years old. He saw my wheelchair.

"Are you him?" he asked.

"No. But he will be coming around the corner really soon," I answered.

He dug into his pants pocket and pulled out two five-dollar bills and some coins.

"This is all I have in my piggy bank. Would you give it to him?"

I had a better idea. "Why don't you wait and give it to him yourself?"

The young man nodded. A few minutes later, Rick came by and stopped to shake hands with him and thank him.

"See what Rick is doing?" Jim asked. "He's making it cool to be around disabled people."

The next afternoon was beautiful and sunny. While Rick was having lunch in his motorhome, Jim parked me behind it and went off the beaten path to pick chokecherries.

A car slowed down when I was at the motorhome. The woman driving got out with three children and came over to me.

"We are so proud of you," she said, shaking my hand. "You sure have gone a long way."

And then it dawned on me: they thought I was Rick.

"Good luck for the rest of your tour. We really hope you get to Vancouver safely."

They gave me $32. Before they drove away, another car stopped and the same thing happened. I saw Rick in the back window of the motorhome, shaking his fist at me before a big smile crossed his face. By the time he finished lunch, my mistaken-identity take had reached $85 for the donation pail.

The response was a tribute to the people of Newfoundland, who in a way were responsible for making the Man in Motion World Tour a success. Because what the ever-smiling Rick and his tour companions weren't saying was a well-hidden fact—in terms of raising funds, the trip had thus far been a failure.

The Newfies didn't know that. They knew only that they wanted to help. So, in the province that was known as the nation's poverty pocket, they dug down and gave what they could— nickels, dimes, quarters and, in one case, a pan of freshly baked blueberry muffins from an elderly woman who said, "I don't have any money, but I wanted to give something."

Across the Maritimes, the reaction was the same, and the word was spreading. It is no coincidence that when the tour reached Ottawa, Brian Mulroney dropped a $1-million cheque into a fundraising basket. Across Canada, people were sensing that something big was happening, and reaching for bills and chequebooks.

Jim and I did some good work in our time in Newfoundland. We travelled with the tour to Clarenville, two hundred kilometres northwest of St. John's. We booked into the same hotel as Rick and just as we finished filing one story, the telephone in our room rang. It was Rick, inviting Jim and me to his room, since we were flying back to Edmonton the next day.

We talked about friends in wheelchair basketball. Rick opened up about his romance with physiotherapist Amanda Reid, which really wasn't public knowledge, and said I could write the story. Amanda talked about it, too, which filled the story out.

The next morning, Jim and I followed the tour for an hour

before we had to drive to St. John's to catch our flight home. Rick stopped wheeling to say goodbye on the highway.

"Here, I have something for you," he said, and gave me a pair of his gloves from the tour. I was very touched.

Jim and I celebrated his fiftieth birthday with some single malt Scotch on the flight home. I had my laptop with the seven-line display and wrote the Rick–Amanda love story on the way to Edmonton.

I called Rick every few weeks as he wheeled west through Nova Scotia, Prince Edward Island and Quebec. Thunder Bay, Ontario, was a key stop for him because it was there that his dear friend Terry Fox had to end his one-legged run across Canada in 1980, one year before his death, as the cancer beat his body, although it could never beat his heart. Rick was to visit the Terry Fox monument there, and he sent me with photographer Chris Schwartz to capture the story.

Chris and I were within five feet of Rick when he wheeled up to the Fox monument. I wanted to give him his privacy and let him have his moment with Terry, but since I was there to cover it, I couldn't.

We went back to the Valhalla Inn to file our story. Nothing worked. Chris had a new machine to transmit his pictures. No matter what he tried or how vehemently he cursed, it wouldn't function. He almost chucked it out the hotel window.

I wasn't having much better luck with my laptop. I had no problem writing the story, but I could not connect to the *Journal* newsroom. The two rubber couplers to place the phone receiver in for the transmissions would not make the connection. Chris and I tried for ninety minutes. Nothing.

Meet Jim Taylor. I began reading Jim's sports columns in the *Vancouver Sun* in my late teens and was a big fan. Jim wrote the book on the tour and we started a great friendship when he was in Newfoundland. I called him and explained the problem. He came to our room, looked at the laptop and wished me luck.

The *Journal* was starting to call for my story because they were considering it for the front page and wanted to get it out to the rest of the newspaper chain. I couldn't file.

I called Jim in a panic.

"Bring that piece of crap to my room and I will read your piece back to the *Journal*," he offered.

"What's your favourite drink?" I asked.

"Martinis," said Jim.

"What's your favourite number?"

"Seven, I guess," he answered.

I called the hotel's room service and ordered seven martinis to Jim's room, packed up my laptop, hauled it to his room, and sat there as one of my newspaper mentors read my story, line for line, to the *Journal* rewrite desk. Jim could have made editorial changes but he didn't, something I will always cherish.

He was halfway through dictating my story when the martinis showed up. I hope he enjoyed them.

When the tour crossed the Alberta–Saskatchewan border in late February, I caught up to it again. The *Journal* sent three of us—photographers Jim Cochrane and Chris Schwarz and me—for the first few days of Rick's time in Alberta. It was very exciting for me to have him in my own province.

There are many stories from the road I will never forget. We rolled into Bow Island, a small town in Alberta between Medicine Hat and Lethbridge. When we asked for a 5:00 a.m. wake-up call, the motel desk clerk gave us two alarm clocks.

When the tour headed north to Edmonton from Calgary, I really started feeling the pressure of keeping on top of things. The *Edmonton Sun* had assigned a reporter to cover the tour as well, giving me some competition. Rick's road crew—especially Mike Reid and Donnie Alder—had my back, though. With the increased coverage, Rick had media availability after every rest break before he carried on wheeling. Mike and Donnie made sure I was always situated in my chair right in front of the motorhome before Rick came out. When we were in Innisfail, Alberta, just south of Red Deer, my parents drove from Edmonton to meet us. It was a great feeling to introduce them to Rick and Amanda.

I hit a low point when we hit Hobbema, about an hour south of Edmonton. There were five hundred people at the evening event in a gymnasium. At the end of Rick's speech, the reporters gathered around him. I was on the other side of the gym and there was no way I could wheel through the crowd. Jim Cochrane was in the scrum and I was on my own.

Panic set in. What if Rick said something big? What if he was hurt and needed a few days off? What if he thought Alberta was the best leg of the tour? What if... ? Overtired and overwhelmed, I wheeled up against one of the walls of the gymnasium with tears in my eyes.

As I watched Rick being interviewed by all the Edmonton media—and not being able to be there—I thought I couldn't do it anymore. Five minutes went by. And then I saw one of the Hobbema elders who had made a special presentation to Rick. There was an opportunity, I thought. I wheeled up to him, intro-duced myself and asked him for his impressions of Rick and the tour.

He told me he had presented Rick with a special feather, which was only meant for senior elders of the Hobbema band. He gave me great detail and was a wonderful storyteller. I went back to my hotel room and wrote a story no one else had.

Edmonton was a rest period before Rick headed west on the Yellowhead Highway to Jasper. He had only a few public appearances—one being shooting pucks with Edmonton mayor Laurence Decore before an Edmonton Oilers game. The rest of the time, he laid low in his downtown hotel room. Off the record, I was told that Wayne Gretzky had taken Rick out one night after a hockey game. I thought about crashing the party, then thought again.

Mom cooked a turkey the night before the tour left Edmonton and had the entire road crew over for a home-cooked meal. We had a great time. Rick and Amanda politely excused themselves for a bit of alone time before the big push to Vancouver.

I covered the tour until it hit the British Columbia border. I had learned never to trust Glenn de Goeij, the RCMP member who escorted Rick throughout Alberta. When we were in Edmonton, one night Glenn took one of my drinking straws and secretly poked a hole in it, so when I took a drink I got nothing. It became a standing joke for the rest of the time we were in Alberta. Every day, at one point, Glenn sabotaged my straw and performed minor surgery.

When Rick wheeled into Vancouver to end his 34-country journey, the *Journal* decided not to send me. I went on my own dime and took Randy Kilburn. It was neat to see Rick cross the finish line. And in the fall of 1986, I had the honour of being invited to Rick and Amanda's wedding in Vancouver. I sat beside musician David Foster—who wrote the Man in Motion theme—who bet me twenty dollars Rick would walk in on crutches to meet Amanda. I thought he would use his trade-mark chair and wheel in. When the wedding ended, I had to reach for my wallet and pay up, but there was one memorable wheelchair moment.

The newlyweds did the traditional wedding waltz with Amanda sitting in Rick's lap, arms around his neck, as they wheeled around the floor to the music of the group Boston playing (what else?) "Amanda." It was moving and loving and wonderful. Then one of Rick's hometown buddies from Williams Lake, BC, shouted good-naturedly, "Do a wheelie!"

We saw Rick's head turn slightly to whisper something into Amanda's ear. The message, as we found out later, was "Freeze!"

Then he leaned back, threw the front wheels into the air, and completed the dance on the big back wheels only.

Jim Taylor, the anxious author, asked him about it later.

"Were you out of your mind?" he asked diplomatically. "One slip, and there goes the honeymoon."

Rick had a simple answer.

"The man challenged me," he said.

And that is my friend, Rick Hansen.

19
·····

"What Are You Doing Monday?"

I t is the most agonizing, gut-wrenching assignment in newspapers: interviewing parents who've just lost a child. In the spring of 1985, three months into my new dream job as full-time reporter for the *Journal*, I drew the short straw.

Wherever possible, I prefer person-to-person interviews. It's much easier to establish a rapport when you're face to face, and easier to see whether you're being lied to or just fed a line. But the real problem is my voice, which can be difficult to understand. This time, there was no getting around it.

I was working the 2–10 p.m. shift in the newsroom. We were writing a story on the need for tougher safety regulations for baby seats, and needed a voice to speak out. Ian Williams, a veteran police reporter, had the telephone number of a family whose four-month-old baby had been killed. My job was to phone them.

I stared at the phone number a good minute before I called.

"Hi, my name is Cam Tait and I am a reporter with the *Edmonton Journal*," I began.

"You asshole," said the man at the other end of the line. "What bar are you in? You're drunk, aren't you? Don't you know what our family has been through? How dare you!"

"I am very sorry about your loss," I said. "I am a reporter with the *Edmonton Journal* and—"

"What bar are you in?" he demanded, clearly angry and outraged. "I'm going to come down and take a round out of you right now."

Small beads of sweat turned into pools on the top of my forehead. Desperately, I tried again.

"Sir, I am very sorry. But I am not trying to make things any worse than they already are," I said.

"What do you know about hardship?" he demanded.

I was in trouble. I looked up. Ian had just hung up his telephone. I put my hand over the mouthpiece and quickly explained the situation. He came over to my desk and explained my situation to the gentleman on the other end of the line. After a minute, he gave me back the telephone.

"Hello?" I said very nervously.

"Sir," the voice at the other end began, "I am very, very sorry. We have had some prank calls since our son's death and it has been very hard."

He then gave me a 45-minute interview, and really shared many of his heartfelt feelings of how he was missing his son. I felt he wanted—and needed—to talk.

Sometimes, I feel really sorry for the people I interview. It is a double whammy because many people are nervous talking to a reporter, and even more people are nervous about speaking to someone with a disability. Again, I rely on humour to break the ice with one of the first questions I ask: "Do you have a good lawyer? Because you never know what might end up in the newspaper."

Conducting interviews over the telephone can be a little tricky. If someone can see me in my chair, perhaps they brace themselves for my speech pattern. But when they hear my voice for the first time over the telephone, it can be a little intimidating. But there was one instance when I was very thankful to be working over the telephone. I covered the United Way campaign in Edmonton for several years and wrote a story about their member agencies. One of them was the Elizabeth Fry Society, an agency that helps convicted female offenders re-enter society. After a 20-minute phone interview with one woman, I asked her why she was in jail.

"Murder," she said.

Oh.

● ● ●

My path to full-time employment with the *Journal* was, to put it mildly, circuitous.

In my work with *The Spokesman*, I was getting information about wheelchair sports events in Edmonton. I wrote an advance story for an upcoming wheelchair track meet and mailed it to George Ward, purely on spec as he'd specified that memorable night with Rimmer. On August 18, 1979, it became my first-ever story in the *Journal*. But on-spec work didn't put groceries on the table. To do that, I went into full scramble.

My sports writing at *The Spokesman* turned into a full-time job in late 1980. *The Spokesman* received government funding to hire a writer, which saw my salary increase to $880 a month. I covered sports, news and features. But I wanted more. As a faithful Rimstead fan, I saw how humour could be very effective if it was used the right way. I wanted to try my hand at being funny in print, so I pitched an idea to Larry for a humour column called The Great Debate With Tait. Larry bought the idea and we put it on the back page of the paper.

And we had fun with it. I wrote about some of the antics I took part in, like washing my hair in the rain, and running for mayor of Edmonton but announcing my candidacy at a conference in Calgary. Perhaps the Great Debate that received the most feedback was the one I wrote on drinking straws—and how adult beverages needed a different straw, depending on the drink. Of course, I gave specific examples. A milkshake straw was suggested for drinking beer, while a sipping drink—Scotch on the rocks—needed a very narrow straw. I ended the piece with: "Gee, I wrote an entire column on straws. I wonder if it sucks."

Mom and Dad bought me a pocket tape recorder for Christmas, which made interviews easier. I'd developed my own form of shorthand with a pen and notepad, but my handwriting caused many people to wonder if I could, in fact, read my own writing. Some people I interviewed were more interested in the way I was taking notes than answering my questions. I made key words large to tell me that was important, and used smaller print for secondary things. Sometimes I wrote down only two or three words on a page, but that told me they were important. I am fortunate to have quite a good memory, pretty close to photographic. I had to remember things like phone numbers because it was easier to remember them than to write them down.

The tape recorder was good, but just for feature interviews when I had more time to transcribe tape. It was very time consuming to turn the tape recorder on, play ten to fifteen seconds of tape, turn the tape off and then type the quote. It really slowed me down if I was working on a deadline. Luckily, most of my work was for *The Spokesman*, which was a monthly.

It was all valuable experience, but when *The Spokesman* went through a shakeup, I bailed—and the bouncing began. I took a public relations job with the Alberta Committee of Consumer Groups of Disabled Persons, a lobby group, publicly creating awareness for people with disabilities, which, since I was no longer covering wheelchair sports, put an end to my *Journal* freelancing. But I got to use my NAIT radio training and wrote a series of radio spots on general awareness about people with disabilities. They were aired on radio stations throughout the province.

One of my favourite projects was a slide-tape presentation I wrote and produced, a neat collection of snippets of songs to go with pictures of the point we were trying to make. The slide presentation showed me going through my day, and showed how communities could make their environments more inclusive for people with disabilities. At the end of the housing section, the slide was me sitting in front of the fence of the Fort Saskatchewan jail; at the end of the transportation section, I was shown on a busy street hitchhiking; when the recreation part ended, a slide popped up of Wayne Gretzky and me facing off at Northlands Coliseum in Edmonton.

My job also gave me a small glimpse of how government works. I often went to Question Period at the Alberta legislature to keep an ear out if any MLAs talked about disability, and I made frequent day trips by plane to Calgary for meetings. But in the spring of 1982, the board of directors wanted my job to shift focus to make me a fundraiser. I was uncomfortable asking for money. Selling advertising for *The Spokesman* had been strictly a business deal. Fundraising did not sit well with me. And, to be honest, I missed reporting.

So I got my old job back at *The Spokesman*, writing sports and selling advertising—for $700 a month less than I'd been making at the job I'd just quit. Shrewd, Tait. Really shrewd. But I knew now that I wanted my future to be in the newspaper business. Fortunately, I was living at home and although I was paying rent, Mom and Dad were very understanding landlords. Dad said he'd wondered how long it would take me to get back to writing sports—and the answer was eight months.

After yet another shuffle at *The Spokesman* executive level, I was now an assistant editor, writing news and sports, which meant I resumed covering the Northern Lights wheelchair basketball team for our paper and as a *Journal* freelancer, travelling with them up and down the western seaboard of the US. The trips were not without incident.

Roy Sherman was a double amputee, the Lights' tallest player and an inveterate practical joker. We were having dinner at a Mexican restaurant in Dallas when he asked me to close my eyes. I did. Roy then put a whole jalapeno pepper in my mouth, which I swallowed whole. A half hour later, back in my hotel room, I was very sick to my stomach.

But in other ways the team was very helpful. A coach or trainer shared a hotel room with me to help me get dressed in the morning. And I found being around a competitive team like the Lights a motivator for me to do for myself. Some of my best self-dressing techniques were developed in hotel rooms on the road.

And then there was the time our plane landed after a road trip to San Jose. Debbie Shiroshka, the woman I was dating, was sitting in a chair waiting for me at the airport. I was so excited to see her, I made a mad rush, wheeling myself out of customs, backwards as always, without looking over my shoulder to see what was behind me, which was a tradesman, on his hands and knees, laying the final touches to a patch of fresh cement. I wheeled right into it. When Debbie put my wheelchair in her trunk, all four wheels were caked with cement.

An economic slowdown rolled into Edmonton and the *Journal* was making changes. In January 1983, sports editor Marc Horton called me to say the freelance budget had been cut. I had my own column by then and was writing two a week at $100 per, but Marc said his hands were tied. So I focused on *The Spokesman*, writing features for what was now a magazine with me as its editor. I was 23 years old, making $1,500 a month, and I was managing six staff.

Having input into the magazine's layout was really enjoyable and I put my own stamp on the first issue published under my watch.

The provincial government had made quite severe cutbacks to services for people with disabilities. We ran a piece with a few real horror stories of how people with disabilities were afraid of what the future might look like, especially in home care. We had the other side of the story, too, from government—and of course reaction from consumer groups representing people with disabilities.

I knew we needed a strong picture on the magazine's cover to illustrate the story. With the help of my new assistant editor, Bryan Gullion, we took a picture of the legislative building in Edmonton in the background, and had someone's hand cutting a hundred-dollar bill in front of it. The picture certainly got people talking. But my hope was to make them think.

I enjoyed making editorial calls, assigning stories, working with freelance writers and increasing our advertising sales staff. It was fun and the money was decent. So, naturally, when a pie-in-the-sky idea came along, I wheeled away and left it all behind.

Gullion had several years of small newspaper experience. He was a good editor, reporter and a great photographer. We became friends and started sharing a vision of publishing a weekly sports tabloid in Edmonton. The Edmonton Oilers had not sipped from the Stanley Cup yet, but all the signs were pointing in the right direction. Mori LaChapelle, our sales manager, was also gung-ho about starting up a sports paper in town. But when I shared the idea with Mom and Dad, there was a lot of discussion and frowning. It became a very hot topic at the supper table with all of us three kids still living at home. Everyone was adamantly against me starting my own paper, especially when I had just been appointed editor of *The Spokesman*.

Me, I saw it as a chance to cover all sports in Edmonton. Covering wheelchair sports for the *Journal* gave me a taste of how exciting it was. I knew I could never be a beat writer for the Oilers or Eskimos for a daily newspaper, but if I had my own newspaper, it would be easy to assign myself to cover the pros.

My family shot down all of my arguments. I respected their opinion greatly. I just didn't listen to it. At the end of September 1983, I resigned from *The Spokesman* and started October 1 with *Edmonton SportScene*, the name of our paper. Mom knew I was serious when I paid the lawyer's fees to register our company with the $1,500 my grandfather Murray had given me when I was eighteen.

My family wasn't alone in their skepticism. My media friends told me a sports paper in Edmonton had been tried several times before, but nobody could make it go. We didn't listen.

I moved into Bryan's house, where we set up an office. Bryan was the majority partner and he was very generous by hiring me a personal assistant and driver, which made getting to events and practices a lot easier. We did hire one part-time reporter but I did the majority of the writing. And I was busy—we printed a 24-page first edition and ads were slim. Bryan and I were concerned about my byline being on so many of the stories, so we took them off. Several of my buddies who were radio sports reporters wrote columns.

It was great attending hockey games and practices, but I knew by about the third week into it that I had made a mistake. We got three issues out, and then shut down operations. I have never been so mentally and physically exhausted in my life. I moved back home, and while the rest of my family enjoyed a nice turkey dinner at Christmas, I ate crow.

I began 1984 unemployed and living at home. My on-again, off-again freelancing career with the *Journal* was back on again because, for once, my timing was perfect. The paper had just launched a new 12-page Monday sports section, and I caught on as a section columnist, heading to the office each Sunday to produce my effort on one of their computer terminals.

My heart was very heavy one particular Sunday afternoon, the day after the memorial service for my high school buddy, Curtis.

He survived the odds for people with muscular dystrophy but, at the age of 24, he caught pneumonia. It killed him. I was waiting for my ride in the living room of our house and I told Mom I didn't have much energy and didn't know what I was going to write that day.

"Why don't you write about Curtis?" Mom suggested. "He was a big sports fan." I thought about that idea all the way downtown to the *Journal* office. I wrote my 650-word column in thirty-five minutes that day. It came so naturally from the heart. I got a message the next day from a *Journal* editor, saying it read very well and should have been on the front page.

I continued freelancing with the *Journal* and picked up some contract work. I compiled a resource library for Alberta Committee and another for the Alberta Rehabilitation Council for the Disabled—both three-month contracts—and spent some time as an assistant editor for a monthly newspaper put out by the Alberta Council on Aging. But I was spinning my wheels, staying alive but not progressing. There had to be something out there in meaningful work. Something had to happen. And something did.

Managing editor Don Smith called me into his office. A new school for physically disabled kids was opening in Grande Prairie—my hometown—and the *Journal* wanted to send me to cover the story. I jumped at the chance. *Journal* photographer Chris Schwartz and education reporter Cathy Lord returned to the Edmonton International Airport at 6:23 a.m. and headed right to the newsroom to write; Cathy wrote the news story, while I wrote a first-person piece. The next morning, I had my first front-page story.

Maybe it was a job interview. The *Journal* was following the lead of dailies all over the continent and switching from evening to morning. I was in the newsroom preparing my column when assistant editor George Oake asked me into his office. George apologized for not calling me sooner, but he was very busy with the launch of the Sunday newspaper.

"What are you doing Monday?" George asked.

No plans, I told him.

"Good. We're going to get you a telephone and a desk. We would like to hire you as a general reporter in the newsroom. Is the 10:00 a.m. to 6:00 p.m. shift okay with you?"

I was speechless. I asked if he was serious. Yes, he said, he was. George stood up and shook my hand.

I was on cloud nine. I made my way to the sports department and called Mom and Dad to share the news. Sportswriter Allen Panzeri walked by me and overheard my conversation. When I hung up, he asked if the news was true. Was I joining the staff? I told him I was.

"I guess I better sell my stocks in the company," he said before shaking my hand and chuckling. "Congratulations, Tait. You have been waiting for this day for a long time."

● ● ●

Funny, isn't it, how things, good and bad, can come in bunches? My earliest media dreams had involved radio, but I could never get that door open. Newspapers had been my second choice. Now, here I was starting my dream newspaper job—and I had a radio job as well.

Sure, I pushed for it. I was in a wheelchair. Without pushing, I'd never get anywhere. My old NAIT buddy, Gary Chomyn, was promotions manager for 1260 CFRN Radio. Over lunch one day, I pitched him on a two-minute radio editorial that I would write and an announcer would read. CFRN had the radio rights for the Edmonton Oilers. The Northern Lights were starting to become a wheelchair basketball powerhouse and I was covering them almost every day. What if, I asked Gary, we had a weekly wheel-chair sports report?

Gary organized a meeting with Don O'Neil, program director of CFRN, who bought the concept and asked one of the station announcers, Al Coates, to voice it. I mailed my script in every Monday, and Al recorded it to be aired Saturday morning at 10:15. It was fun, but halfway through the summer, I was really struggling to find enough material for one piece a week on wheel-chair sports. My duties at the *Journal* were changing, too. I was writing more news and slowly getting out of sports.

Again, a friend came through for me. Randy Kilburn was named news director of K-97 in 1985. K-97 is an FM rock station that needed to fill an hour of talk programming a day. I met Randy to discuss the idea of doing a 90-second editorial on issues for people with disabilities; he would read my words. Randy then took my idea to radio general manager Terry Stain, who liked the idea, but wasn't completely sold. Terry asked me to do a trial for a month—four editorials—which Randy produced and put on the air. We were trying to rack our brains for a name for the show. One day on the way to work, it hit me just as I turned east on the Whitemud Freeway: Tait Talk was born, and it worked.

I tried to soft-sell the education of disability and fostered a philosophy of working with one another, not against. We wrote one about how certain words can either hamper or diminish the image of disability. For example, I have cerebral palsy, but many people said I suffer from cerebral palsy. Suffer, I think, comes from the medical model that disability is a sickness. The only time I suffer is the morning after the night before, when I've had too many wobbly pops. We did other scripts on accessibility and transportation.

My salary was $300 a month for four editorials, which was fine. But in the fall of 1987, when the station was about to launch a new 60-minute magazine format weekdays, my ambition revved up. I knew I could write five a week; however, five a week on disability might be stretching it. But what if I used it to spread my wings, give opinions on other issues like civic and provincial politics? And, maybe talking about everyday things was a good form of integration. Again, I got the go-ahead, with a minor hiccup. The money would stay the same. It didn't really matter to me. Hell, I would have probably done it for ten dollars a month.

The two jobs made for an interesting schedule. Get up at 5:00 a.m., climb into the bathtub for a shower, get help to finish dressing, grab a quick breakfast, read the *Journal* to find a comment topic, start writing the 300-word piece, send it to the station and catch my ride to the *Journal* newsroom at 8:30 a.m. I really enjoyed the pace—but then, it's a well-known fact that media people are nuts.

In late February 1988, K-97 engineered a fundraising event for the Associated Canadian Travellers, a service group that provided mobility equipment for children and adults with physical disabilities. ACT had a 21-hour telethon to raise funds, so K-97 program director Neil Edwards decided to have a radio marathon from The Brick furniture store in downtown Edmonton, hosted by announcers Stu Jeffries and Bruce Kenyon. A week before the marathon, we taped a television commercial at the store. It had Stu and Bruce in a king-sized bed, explaining that they were trying to get as much sleep as possible before the big show. I came in with a coffee pot at the end of the shot, saying my job was to keep everyone awake.

Ah, yes, television at its finest—but the show went 52 hours and raised $14,000 for ACT. Tait Talk moved to K-97's AM sister station, 930 CJCA, Edmonton's talk radio station at the time. The exposure was greater, and we did make some waves, particularly with one of the station's major advertisers, LaFleche Brothers.

To their credit, LaFleche Brothers organized a fashion show to raise funds for people who sustained burn injuries. When they announced the event, people with burn injuries were recognized but they didn't speak, and they were not part of the program. I didn't agree with that. In fact, I felt sorry for the burn survivors, and thought they were being put on display when they could have really shared their stories and created great awareness. I thought it was another case of business doing something "for" a cause, when it could have done it "with."

So I wrote that and was quite candid. It created a stir with the advertiser, and CJCA program director Rick Lewis called me into his office. He wasn't very happy with my work and asked me not to be so abrasive on the air.

I certainly saw his point. Yet, I knew part of my role was to voice my opinion and, honestly, I didn't care whose feathers I ruffled.

And then there was the elevator caper.

Barrie Harrison—who read my words—got married and the reception was upstairs at the Royal Glenora Club—and there wasn't an elevator. Four strong men carried me up the stairs, and I was grateful. But whenever I'm being carried, I feel my independence and dignity is somewhat depleted. And, before a wedding, the kind folks who carry me haven't had a few adult alcoholic beverages under their belts. It's a different story three or four hours later when they've had a few. It can make for a very interesting ride down.

Two days later, on the Monday, I wrote about those things—and asked if the Royal Glenora would ever install an elevator. Three hours later, the club's general manager, George Pinches, called me at the *Journal*. I thought he was going to chew me out. Instead, he invited me down for a beer that afternoon to ask for advice on installing an elevator. Three months later, we gathered for the official grand opening of the elevator. That was a very gratifying feeling.

I loved writing the show. But, honestly, there wasn't much gas left in the tank when the calendar turned over to 1992. I also didn't want to sound like a broken record, saying the same thing over and over again. In the first week of February 1992, Tait Talk signed off the air.

Neil Edwards invited me to lunch the last day.

"Where would you like to go?" he asked.

"How about the Royal Glenora?" I suggested. "I hear they have an elevator."

20

Flushed with Success

The men's washroom in the newsroom didn't have an enlarged cubicle, but that was okay. I could pull myself up from my chair at a urinal and take care of business. A few months after I started, though, someone in management had the maintenance workers put in a stall large enough for a wheelchair and a grab bar. I didn't ask for one. Hell, nobody asked me if it would help. It just… appeared.

That, in a nutshell, was the *Journal*'s approach to my disability as it related to my job. In terms of workload and quality expectations, nothing had changed since George Ward had offered me that first freelancing job when I wheeled Rimmer to his table in the hotel lobby—get the assignment and do quality work— which was exactly how I wanted it. But where assistance could be provided, it would be, and was.

Take out-of-town assignments. I could get around Edmonton on my own via taxi, but road trips posed challenges for my personal care. I needed someone to help me with my shoes and socks, closing my pants and buttons. And, oh yeah, packing. I can't pack a suitcase to save my soul.

In 1985 the paper approved my travelling to Vancouver for a national rehabilitation conference on some groundbreaking technology and new thinking for people with physical disabilities. A staff member working in the group home where I was living said she would come to help me. I assumed it was my responsibility to pay for her expenses—something I was happy to do. I asked the *Journal* to book two flights for me and provided my credit card to pay for my attendant's fare. Later that same day, assistant managing editor Linda Hughes—who later became publisher—came over to my desk.

"If we're going to send you on the road, and you need help, we'll pay for someone to go with you," she said, and gave me back the card.

I was overwhelmed. And it felt damn good to have the paper supporting me like that. And it continued—helped to no end by caring photographers like Jim Cochrane and Chris Schwartz, who were with me for the Man in Motion coverage.

After the Hansen tour, I didn't travel much with the *Journal*, but whenever I did, I had company. In 1991, when I went to Calgary to meet former White House press secretary James Brady, another *Journal* photographer, Ed Kaiser, was my roommate and my assistant. After our marriage, my wife, Joan, travelled with me for some news and sports assignments—Red Deer, Alberta; Weyburn, Saskatchewan; Portland, Oregon... hey, honey, didn't I say we'd see the world?

Sure, my work came with problems. Doesn't everyone's? But more often I found confirmation of my belief in human kindness.

Difficult press box accessibility at the junior hockey arena when I was covering the Edmonton Oil Kings? Jordi Weidman of the Kings made arrangements for me to sit on the top level of the concourse, with a small table and an extension cord for my laptop.

Technological problems? Oh, yeah. I used a tape recorder to get my interviews. The only time-consuming issue was taking my hands off the keyboard to start the tape, listening to the quote, stopping the tape and then typing it in. But—thank you, Bluetooth—in later years, I sent the audio file right to my laptop. That allowed me to stop and start the audio with the keys on my computer, which speeded things up considerably.

But technology was a two-edged sword. Somehow, the faster the technology worked, the earlier the deadlines got. (In his days at the Vancouver *Province*, Jim Taylor pasted a sign on his laptop: If We Get Any Effing Faster, We'll be a Weekly!) When I first started covering Junior A hockey in 2005, the deadline for the first edition was 11:15 p.m. I had plenty of time to craft a good game story, and I filed it twenty minutes after the game, which was roughly 9:40 p.m. I then went to the dressing rooms to get quotes and rewrote much of the first story for the home edition.

With the first-edition deadline now 10:30 p.m., I had to file five minutes after the final whistle, pack my laptop, then head down to the dressing room for interviews and work from the media room on the ground floor.

Clearly, I needed an assist.

I met with Laura Budzak, an occupational therapist, who assisted me with my overall home care program at the condo where Joan and I were living. I asked for extra hours to pay for a personal attendant to help me in the field—setting up my laptop, and wheeling me to the washroom and down to the dressing rooms, especially since time was an issue. Laura went to bat for me with her supervisor and got me an additional 110 hours per month at $16 an hour from the provincial government funding to pay someone to accompany me to games.

The job was shared by Denise Bionjeaux, who did a wonderful job getting me showered and dressed in the morning and accepted an additional part-time position to help me get around Rexall Place, and Rhonda Ferguson, a first-year University of Alberta student who was volunteering in the Oil Kings' media lounge

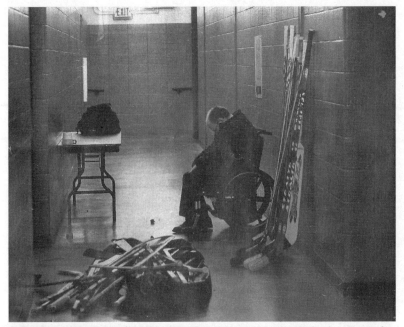

It may lack the glamour of the NHL, but reporting on junior hockey was a fun experience for me, especially with the Edmonton Oil Kings in 2008.

before the games. It didn't hurt that she was a big hockey fan whose father, Ron, worked as a scout for the Carolina Hurricanes out of his Red Deer home. Denise and Rhonda gave me increased independence by helping me with setting up my laptop, getting tea for me to drink between periods, walking up the stands to get someone I wanted to interview, packing up my laptop after the game and wheeling me down to the dressing rooms for post-game quotes. Because of their assistance, I could cover four or five games a week and meet those confounding deadlines.

So, the big things were being taken care of. But for people with disabilities, it's often the little things that can do you in. For instance, taxis.

I used the Disabled Adult Transportation System to get back and forth from home to the newsroom. But back in the 1980s, DATS couldn't be used very much for same-day requests. I had to book a day ahead for a trip, and since it was a shared system, there could be up to an hour's wait. To get back to the *Journal* to write my story, I used cabs. Frankly, that scared me a little because, depending upon the driver and his attitude toward the chair and the person in it, I could be left in minor to serious trouble.

Don't get me wrong. I have had some wonderful drivers over the years. Having the same driver—or even two—really helped things. There were no surprises, for them or me. Wherever you are, Robert, Garth, Tony, Andy, Ernie, Julie, Walter, Wally, Marwann, Hussein and Ali, I thank you. You went out of your way to get the job done. But there were occasional exceptions.

In December 1992, I went to cover a Salvation Army fundraiser called the Santa Shuffle in Hawrelak Park in Edmonton. It ended at one o'clock, so I called a cab to take me home. As usual, I identified myself and said I was in a wheelchair, something Yellow Cab had on file, then told everyone I had a ride on the way and they could lock the door to the shack used for the event. But since it was eighteen below and windy and I'd be the only person left in the park, long-time *Journal* cartoonist Yardley Jones insisted on staying with me. Thank goodness.

In five minutes, the cab pulled up in front of us and I thanked the driver for coming. He popped the trunk for my wheelchair and I staggered into the front seat.

"Where do you want to go?" he asked in broken English. I gave him my address.

"No, I don't want to take you there. Get out of my cab," he said. "Get out now."

He got out of the car, unloaded my wheelchair, opened my door and put me in my chair, and then drove away. Luckily, Yardley was still with me. If I didn't have my cellphone with me, things could have been much worse. Another cab came within ten minutes and I arrived home safely, but a little cold.

I reported the driver to the cab company. The next morning at six o'clock, Yellow Cab manager Bob Findlay called and met me that morning at the *Journal* to make sure I was okay. Bob fired the driver, who, sadly, suffered from depression.

Sometimes, though, the only factor in transportation mishaps is stupidity, which is, of course, a two-way street. In 2005, I made a trip to Bonnyville with the Fort Saskatchewan Traders. My cab driver, Wally, drove me to the Fort Saskatchewan arena, where four players helped me walk from the cab onto the bus. I never sat in my wheelchair. When we arrived, I asked the bus driver to get my chair.

"What wheelchair?" he asked. "I never loaded any wheelchair."

At that moment, my cellphone rang. It was Joan. "What's wrong with this picture?" she asked. "You're in Bonnyville. Your cab driver just showed up at the condo with your wheelchair. How can that be?"

Because I had walked onto the bus, we'd forgotten about my chair in the cab's trunk. So the bus went one way, and the cab with my chair went the other. Again, people came through. A few of the players walked me into the arena, then walked over to the Bonnyville hospital and borrowed a wheelchair for the evening.

● ● ●

My years at the *Journal* started with general assignments for the news side and wheelchair sports for the sports section. On my first day, I saw Don Smith leaving for lunch and quietly asked him what my salary was. I'd been so elated to get the job that I'd never brought up the subject. If he'd said, "You work free, but we provide hamburgers and coffee," I'd probably have nodded and asked, "Where do I sign?"

Don took a pen, grabbed a notepad from a desk and wrote down a figure: $511 a week, or $2,000-plus a month—the most

I had ever made. I was living in a group home in the west end, paying $240 a month for room and board. Did I have it made, or what?

I quickly realized reporters' best stories are ones they come up with themselves. Very seldom did the assignment I snatched out of my mailbox in the morning make the front page of the city section. Then assignment editor Dave Cooper showed me the new Edmonton white pages, which had a listing of Edmonton businesses that claimed to be wheelchair accessible. I knew many on that list were not. *Journal* photographer Chris Schwartz surveyed the city, checking out the places that were actually inaccessible. I was given the green light to write a first-person piece—something I discovered was a perk. To go along with my story, Chris caught a picture of me jammed between the washroom door and the wall in an establishment listed as being accessible. The story got good play and made solid impact. Nobody was writing on disability issues in Edmonton on a regular basis. And there it was—my reporting niche.

I wrote about people with disabilities—feature stories and issues like employment and transportation. Publisher William Newbigging was a strong supporter of the United Way campaign. City editor Wendy Koenig took me for coffee and said she wanted me to profile every one of the forty-two member agencies during the campaign. I found the work very rewarding. It reaffirmed my belief in the importance of volunteers in the community, something I'd learned first-hand as a young child.

My only concern was the danger of becoming stereotyped— the guy with the disability writing only about people facing the same challenges. The *Journal* didn't let it happen. For two years in the late 1980s, I wrote Junior *Journal*, a weekly column for kids, featuring my own creation, a character named Uncle Pete who did all kinds of things. In fact, Uncle Pete really wanted to go water skiing one summer day, but couldn't find a lake with a hill in it.

In the summer of 1991, *Journal* editor Murdoch Davis moved me into the features department. I liked that because I could take my time flushing a story out, and not worry about daily deadlines. In the fall, he added a new column for me called Giving. It ran every Thursday, a roundup of the charity scene that drew so much information that it was bumped to twice a week until the Christmas season was over.

I had a great job. I wrote one column and two feature stories a week until 1998, when I pitched an idea to features editor Doug Swanson to write three columns a week on community events and volunteers. With the invention of email, we named the column Ourcommunity.cam, a play on the dot-com thing. My aim was to show readers where their fundraising efforts went. After writing about an upcoming event, I tried to report how much money it raised and how that money was put to use. I called it investment and kept track of funds raised, adding them up at the end of every column. It was a joy to write, because I could put my own personal spin on it. And it was rather unique. How many people in the newspaper business could say they wrote about good news on a daily basis?

There's another perk to being in the newspaper business: you get to meet celebrities. Veteran reporters can become blasé about it, or at least pretend to ("Sinatra? Yeah, I met him. Nice guy."). Maybe I wasn't in that end of the business long enough...

October 17, 1987—From the first time I heard Stevie Wonder sing "My Cherie Amour" when I was ten, I wanted to meet him. When I was a member of a youth group in my teens, we always ended the night by playing "You Are the Sunshine of My Life." Stevie Wonder was coming to Edmonton as part of a tour. I was doing some regular work for K-97, the radio station that was bringing him to town. This was my chance! I asked program director Neil Edwards if I could interview him after the show.

One of the great bonuses of the newspaper biz: getting to meet your heroes. For me, meeting and speaking to Stevie Wonder in 1987 was an unforgettable moment.

He agreed to put in the request, but suggested I shouldn't bet the mortgage on meeting him.

But, somehow, there I was, waiting by the freight elevator in Northlands Coliseum as instructed, to meet my singing hero. And here he came, in the middle of a five-large-men protective circle. The concert promoter introduced me to him. After the interview, I was told that Mr. Wonder had not been informed that I have cerebral palsy. Yet, when he heard my voice, he immediately bent down onto his knees so he was at the same eye level as me, his hands gently searching for the wheels on my chair. I thought that was amazing, to have the presence of mind to be at my level, even though he could not see me. I found it interesting that he always had a hand on a member of his security guards, always knowing exactly where he was. In the five minutes I had with him, I asked him what the key was for someone with a disability to be in high profile.

"We are the chosen ones," he said, putting his arm out, trying to find my neck, and then giving me a bear hug. "And we have a responsibility to show the world what can be done."

The following Monday I wrote my experiences for K-97. At the end of my comments, we faded in Stevie Wonder's song, "There's a Place in The Sun."

● ● ●

January 22, 1990—*Edmonton Journal* photographer Ed Kaiser and I were sitting in the lobby of the Westin Hotel in Calgary when a young PR man brought the word.

"Mr. Brady is waiting for you," he said. "I should warn you, though. He isn't feeling that well today. He might only be able to give you ten or fifteen minutes."

I nodded as we made our way into the elevator. Ten minutes with James Brady, the former White House press secretary, in Calgary to speak—with terrifying expertise—at a black-tie fundraising dinner in support of people with brain injuries? I gave the journalism gods a silent thank you.

The *Journal* sent me to interview him about living with a brain injury and the work he was doing with gun control. Brady sustained his injury in 1981 during an attempted assassination of US president Ronald Reagan. The bullet aimed for Reagan hit Brady in the back of the head. Emergency surgery saved his life.

Ed and I were led into his suite and met by Brady's wife, Sarah. I wheeled up to Brady's wheelchair and extended my hand for a handshake. He ignored it.

"Is that your wheelchair?" he asked, taking a good, hard look at it.

"Yes, sir, it is," I said.

"Do me a favour," he said. "Don't fall out of it."

There was an awkward silence before a smile washed over his face, followed by a quiet chuckle. He reached for my hand and shook it.

"Jim Brady," he said. "Nice to meet you."

Sarah sat down beside him on the couch. "I should let you know: Jim likes to tease people. Just be ready," she said.

I knew I had to be fairly quick with my questions since his public relations person had said he wasn't feeling well. He was very generous with his answers and described the shooting in specific detail. Every few minutes he would get stuck on one word and repeat it over and over. His brain injury affected his thought process, almost like a record player making an LP skip. When it happened, Sarah tapped him on the shoulder or said, "Okay, Jim. Carry on." Brady stopped speaking and gathered his thoughts— and then resumed.

He had a name for almost everyone, and talked about his tough rehabilitation after his injury. "I was sure worked hard by those physical terrorists," he said, before his wife corrected him. "He means physiotherapists."

Former White House press secretary James Brady and his wife Sarah were gracious and informative during a Calgary stop on his speaking tour in 1991. Severely wounded during the attempted assassination of president Ronald Reagan ten years earlier, Brady became a leader in the fight for gun control.

"My wife and I are the dog and pony show," he said several times. "I'll let you figure out who's who."

Brady wanted to know about me and my job, especially since he was a former reporter. We started joking back and forth about our disabilities. Half an hour into the interview, his public relations person reminded Brady of the time and that there were five more reporters waiting for him the hallway.

"And who do you work for?" Brady asked.

"You, sir," the young man said.

"I am having fun with this gentleman. Tell 'em to wait until I'm ready."

We talked and laughed for another fifteen minutes until I thought I had better end things.

"Tell you what," Brady said. "You make yourself down to Washington DC and I will take you for lunch at the White House."

One day...

We shook hands and he smiled.

"Thanks for not falling out of your chair for me."

Ed and I walked out of the suite and got some dirty looks from television reporters who were patiently waiting. I didn't care; James Brady was one of those interviews you just don't ever forget.

Things couldn't get much better. But deep down I'd always wanted to get back into the sports department. In 2003, I asked sports editor John MacKinnon if I could write a weekly column on amateur sports. And in June 2003, Tait on Tuesday began in the sports section. Seven months later, at my request, I moved into the sports section full-time. The first assignment was shadowing the cast and crew of *Hockey Night in Canada* at an Edmonton Oilers game for a half-page feature story.

There was no NHL season because of a work stoppage so I pitched a weekly column on Junior A hockey, taking me back to my Edmonton Crusader days. With Junior A teams an hour's driving distance of Edmonton, there were lots of stories to be told. Edmonton didn't have a Western Hockey League back then— the closest team was Red Deer, a 90-minute drive. I covered the Red Deer Rebels and the Medicine Hat Tigers in the first round of playoffs. Now, for the first time in my life, I was writing game stories on deadlines. I knew now what heaven looked like: it was a hockey arena, and I was a *pro tem* angel.

21

Hangin' with 99

February 4, 1989—The *LA Times, Philadelphia Inquirer, CBS Sports, NBC Sports* and other media had gathered around the corner stall of the Los Angeles Kings' dressing room in a semicircle, looking for the first quote from Wayne Gretzky. The Kings had just played Gretzky's old team, the Edmonton Oilers, in the Great Western Forum and the media wanted answers. Wayne saw me outside the semicircle and stood up.

"Could the rest of you wait for a minute? I need to talk to Cam from Edmonton," Wayne said. "Cammie, get in here. Got your tape recorder working? Let's do this."

I felt kind of bad knowing other reporters were on deadline for the late-night news in a few hours as well as the next day's paper. But I jumped at the chance, as everyone did, to talk to Wayne. He had a friend back in Edmonton who had leukemia and needed a bone marrow transplant. Earlier that day at the Kings' morning skate, Wayne asked me if I would write a story in the *Journal* that might help the cause. I was in Los Angeles on a little holiday and didn't have any reporting gear. I made a quick shopping trip to buy a small pocket recorder.

So while all the other reporters in the room anxiously looked at their watches every thirty seconds with their looming deadlines, Wayne talked to me about his friend, how he wanted to help and where people could donate.

It was a heartfelt story. And, more importantly, Wayne was answering my questions. Because, for years, he couldn't understand a word I said.

I first met Wayne in July 1979. He was at a reception the night before a charity softball game and I went as a *Spokesman* reporter. I wasn't using a tape recorder then and had my trusty notebook and pen.

I wheeled up to Wayne, introduced myself and asked if I could ask him a few questions. He had a confused look on his face and then, very gently, took my notepad and pen from me.

"I would be thrilled to give you my autograph," he said in kindness. "Who do I make it to?"

I explained myself. This time, he looked even more confused.

Wayne turned to Herman Wierenga, a colleague from *The Spokesman* who was at the event with me.

"What did he say?"

Herman repeated what I had said, and Wayne agreed to answer my questions. He couldn't understand me, so Herman kindly acted as my interpreter.

Over the next couple of years, I'd run into Wayne after Oilers games, where we'd exchange hellos and not much else. In 1982, he played in a floor hockey game with kids with mental disabilities. I arranged an interview outside the Oilers' dressing room to publicize it. My NAIT buddy, Gerry Postma, was with me. I posed my first question, Wayne got that old confused look on his face, and just like that, we were doing a rerun from 1979, with Gerry playing Herman.

"What did he say?" Wayne asked him, and Gerry played interpreter the rest of the way.

But that all changed in December 1981—the night Wayne scored his fiftieth goal of the season in the Oilers' thirty-ninth game.

In the dressing room post-game, I overheard someone saying that Wayne was celebrating the record at a downtown restaurant called Fingers. As my cousin, Cam Traub, and I were pulling out of the parking lot, I casually suggested we stop for a quick bite to eat at Fingers. I didn't tell Cam who might be dropping by.

We were just finishing up when Wayne entered with about ten friends. Five minutes or so later, two shot glasses of tequila were delivered to our table from Wayne, with two straws. Cam and I drank them and thanked Wayne on our way out. At least, we thought that was what we were doing. Wayne had other ideas.

"Cammie, good to see you," he said. "Please join us. Why don't you sit down."

"I already am," I said.

Wayne howled with laughter. We joined the party, and drank everything from beer to Dom Perignon. More importantly, we communicated—something, I think, that began with a laugh. Cam and I shared two hours with Wayne that night. We got to know one another, and it stuck.

I wasn't sure it would. But I was sitting at the next Oilers' practice after they returned from an eastern swing road trip when Wayne came off the ice five minutes before the rest of the team, as he often did, and spied me.

"Cammie, you jerk. How are you?" he asked. "I have to have a whirlpool right now and I feel like being bored, so why don't you come talk to me?"

I was no longer the guy in the wheelchair he could not understand. I was one of the boys he could poke fun at. We weren't buddies, but we were friends.

The spring of 1984 in Edmonton was electric, with the Oilers winning their first Stanley Cup, beating the New York Islanders. A few days after the big championship game, I was invited to a celebration dinner downtown hosted by the City of Edmonton, where Wayne invited me for brunch that Sunday with his girlfriend,

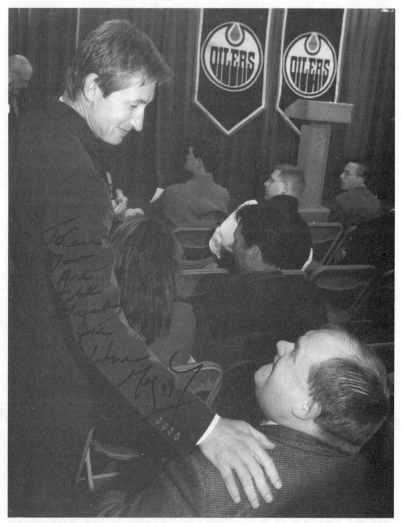

Wayne Gretzky's life as an Edmonton Oiler was ever-hectic, but never too busy for him to stop to say "Hi." Over the years, that's never changed.

Vicki Moss, which was planned for a restaurant but wound up as a home-cooked brunch, prepared by Vicki's mom, Sophie.

Wayne had just had minor surgery on his ankle and excused himself for a little post-lunch nap. "See what you do to me, Cammie?" he asked. "You put me to sleep."

While Wayne had a little siesta, Vicki and Mrs. Moss and I had a great visit. Wayne woke up and offered to drive me home. He had just won a new car for his play in the Stanley Cup finals—a convertible Mercedes Benz, with a very small trunk. After Wayne got me seated in the front seat, he struggled for five minutes getting my wheelchair into the trunk.

The trip provided a small glimpse of Wayne's hectic life as a superstar. Whenever we stopped at a red light, people recognized him and started waving. Some even got out of their cars in the middle of the intersection to get a closer look. Wayne always smiled and waved and never seemed wearied by it, although there must have been times when he craved some alone time. But he parked in the driveway of my parents' home, where I was living at the time, unloaded the chair, wheeled me into the house and met the entire family. Even 84-year-old Grandmother Murray, who always admitted she was never a big hockey fan, came to the front door to shake Wayne's hand.

A few months later, the Wayne Gretzky Golf Classic was held at the Edmonton Country Club. At a reception at the club the night before, Wayne announced that I would play the first hole from my wheelchair to raise funds for the charity the tournament was supporting, construction of a residence for people with mental disabilities.

"Hey, Cammie, I have an idea," he said, playing to the crowd, before looking at me. "Why don't you start now? You might be finished by the time the rest of us tee off tomorrow."

The crowd howled with laughter, and it was so good to know others were laughing with me—and not at me. It would have been a little uncomfortable if Wayne had stood up and told everyone I was playing a hole, and I had cerebral palsy, and wasn't it a novel thing. But putting humour into it made it more personal, more fun.

● ● ●

Now, about the golf...

The game has always fascinated me because it has so many facets: competitive if you're that way inclined; the mental aspect as you try to figure out swing, putting stroke, distance and where the hell the ball went this time; and the social side of things as you gather at the 19th to share drinks, recaps and, shall we say, exaggerations. When I was a kid we went to a few miniature golf courses and I played from my wheelchair. Not all the holes were accessible, but we had fun just the same.

When the International Year of Disabled Persons rolled around in 1981, I wrote a first-person piece about playing one hole of golf, as arranged by my good friend Duncan Harvey at the Glendale Golf and Country Club, where he was a member. "I went golfing last night and shot 36," the story began. "Not bad for one hole. And, at least I knew my handicap."

The first thing you have to do in golfing from a wheelchair is to redefine your definition of distance. Every shot went eight to ten yards. When we reached the green, Duncan very politely asked me if I could step up my short game and putt well. Greenskeepers, he said, weren't that fond of wheelchair marks on putting greens.

I put away my one club, a three-wood driver, until the Gretzky tournament in 1984, when we devised a way for me to help raise money for the charity. But it was a tricky thing. Sponsoring me for, say, a dollar per stroke would turn the thing into a freak show and take the focus away from golf, because the worse I played, the more money I'd raise. The answer? We gave me a 27-stroke handicap on the par-five hole. Sponsors—and I hoped to have a few—would pledge a dollar for every stroke I finished below the handicap. If I finished with twenty, for example, they'd each throw in seven dollars. It gave me the challenge to shoot the best score I could—which would raise more money. Perfect. The difficulty, though, was selling it.

The night before the tournament I was halfway though my sales pitch with Mark Messier when he stopped me. "I didn't bring my slide rule or calculator," Mark said as he dug into his pocket for a crisp one-hundred-dollar bill. "How about we just call it square with this?"

Country club general manager Leo Blindenbach offered to be my agent and manager. I agreed and he circled the room collecting sponsors.

We began the next day with a brunch before the shotgun start at one o'clock. Wayne's agent, Mike Barnett, sent me a pair of golf pants and a shirt from Canadian golfer Jim Nelford—two sizes too small, but I somehow managed to get them on—and Wayne presented me with a blue jacket sporting the tournament logo. Now all I had to do was play.

Wayne came to watch me tee off. My first shot was about five feet. "The crowd pressure got to me," I explained over the laughter. "I'll find my game on the fairway." And I did, finishing with a blazing 6 under my handicap of 27.

I wheeled back to the clubhouse quite happy with my performance. But Leo wasn't through. We spent the afternoon in his golf cart following the tournament, enjoyed the banquet, and then sat in the lobby of the clubhouse, where he lit up a cigar. "Okay," he said, pulling out his trusty envelope and pen. "Now, we take care of business."

As golfers walked from the dinner to the lounge for a drink, Leo told them my score on the first hole. Then he threw out his new line. "It's not too late to support Cam, you know." I had never seen so many hundred-dollar bills in my life. Leo wound up with

ıg for dollars

In golf I was a one-hole wonder, but fellow golfers' generosity and curiosity over how many strokes it would take me to finish the hole became a great charity fundraising gimmick.

$2,800 to add to the charity pot.

I attended Wayne's golf tournament in Edmonton for three more years, including the last one in 1987. He always made sure I felt part of the tournament. Many well-known personalities from across North America attended the event. Thanks to Wayne, I had the pleasure of having cocktails with actors Jamie Farr and Alan Thicke, hockey broadcaster Danny Gallivan, music producer David Foster and Mr. Hockey himself, Gordie Howe.

I was truly gratified by the success of my venture into the world of golf. More importantly, I saw its potential as a fund-raiser for other good causes. In the three years I played in Oiler defenceman Charlie Huddy's tournament, we raised about $2,500 for the Kidney Foundation. As other charities came aboard, we even took the show on the road, the brainchild of golf pro Bill Penny, who'd devised one of the many systems we used over the years to separate backers from their money. They'd bet on my final shot total, and the winner got a new putter, generously donated by the Ping golf people.

Our first stop on what became known as the "Cam Tait Charity Golf Tour" was in Bill's hometown, beautiful downtown Moose Jaw, Saskatchewan, where another hometown boy, Clark Gillies, who won several Stanley Cups with the New York Islanders, held a charity tournament. Bill must have been pretty sure I'd get there—he was walking around the reception the night before the event with five drinking straws sticking out of his back pocket.

I had a great hole, shooting a 15 and, to everyone's surprise, including mine, finishing off by three-putting. Maybe it was my new equipment. Bill had someone in the back of the golf club's pro shop cut down a three-wood driver so I could swing it from a sitting position and get more power behind it than with the regulation-size three-wood I'd used in the past. We also had a putter custom-made like a hockey stick to give me better control, and a golf bag for me that had my name on it.

The hole raised $1,500 for a wonderful cause: a young boy from Moose Jaw needed some surgery to repair damage to his throat. Over the three years of the project, my scores ranged from 31 on a really bad day to—honest to God's truth—a 7, shot at Bill's Pro-Am on the 18th green from the ladies' tee: one shot off the tee, three on the fairway and three putts.

Bill couldn't resist. "Next year, we make things a little more difficult," he said. "We're going to have the Cam Tait Sand Trap Clinic." And he kept his word. Rather than having me play a hole, Bill wheeled me into a sand trap beside the 18th green—right in the middle—and dropped a golf ball.

"Have a good time," he said. "And, if you're still in there when it gets dark, I'll pull my truck around and we'll shine the headlights on you."

We changed the betting, too. Golfers bet how many strokes and how many minutes it took me to get out. The winner had 42 shots and 48 minutes.

One of the side benefits of my golfing career was the way people jumped in to help me improve my game. Take, for instance, Hugh Campbell, the legendary Gluey Hughie of Canadian football fame. In 1987, newly returned to Edmonton to become general manager of the Eskimos, Hugh walked the hole with me and helped me shoot a record 17. To make certain I made the final six-foot putt, he put two of his clubs in a V shape behind the hole. I used my club as a pool cue and the ball made two bounces off Hugh's clubs—and in.

And then there was Kevin Martin, one of the greatest curlers who ever threw a rock, and an avid golfer who can hit the ball a ton. Whenever we were in the same tournament, he walked the hole with me and carried my beverage. And in 1993, we faced a harrowing challenge. On my twelfth shot on a par-five hole, my ball disappeared. Gone.

"How are we going to do this?" he asked me, as seriously as though it was his last rock to win the Brier.

I considered my options and made my decision.

"I need a drink," I said.

Kevin, who was doubling as my caddy, handed me my usual beverage—rye and Coke.

"Good thing I made 'er a triple today, I guess," Kevin said.

"Nobody told me there was a gully in the fairway," I said. "I was at the tee box all day and I couldn't see it. A good caddy would know that."

"Nobody can see it from the fairway, Cam," he growled. "What makes you special? Here, have another drink and hang on. We're goin' in."

So picture this: Kevin wheels me down into this gully, holding me at a 45-degree angle, and I'm swinging a three-wood at this golf ball... in tall grass. It took me eighteen shots to get out of the gully. The triple rye and Coke was gone long before we got to the putting green.

Kevin was also a regular in the Longest Day of Golf foursomes tournament, a fundraiser for the Canadian Cancer Society organized by my friend, Kevin "Shaggy" Shaigec and held annually between 4:00 a.m. and 9:00 p.m. on June 21—the longest day of the year.

I was fortunate enough to be named coach for the Shaigec

team with Kevin Martin, Kevin Hogan and sportscaster Al Nagy for the inaugural in 1991. I had watched Kevin for several years on television as a curler. His post-game interviews turned me on to the game; he made it so engaging and so entertaining. To be able to sit down with him over a bowl of soup and a sandwich and have a visit was a treat and a half.

Kevin is a big kid at heart. When Shaggy, Hogan and I rolled into the parking lot of the Victoria Golf Course in Edmonton a little after 3:30 a.m., Kevin was already on the first tee taking warm-up swings. "Where have you guys been?" he asked. "We have to get going."

The marathon was not without protocol. For example, the guys never drank until the final round, which usually started around 8:00 p.m. Kevin isn't a beer fan so the organizer of the day, Fred Dawson, made sure he had a bottle of rye in the cart.

Of course, after close to sixteen hours of non-stop golf, we could not just go home. We needed to tell stories of the day's events in the lounge upstairs. Naturally, there was no elevator. No matter how tired the guys were, they always had enough energy to haul my wheelchair and me up the three flights of stairs. Going *down* the stairs was a different story.

When the lounge closed, we still couldn't go home. We had to have a nightcap at Earls downtown on Jasper Avenue. As I said, protocol. And that was fine, until the fourth year. Shaggy and Nagy lifted the back side of my chair while Hogan steadied the front. They managed descent of the first set of stairs with no problem. But someone lost grip on the third step of the second set. My chair tipped and I was lying down. The next thing I see is Nagy doing a somersault on my chest before rolling into a heap at the bottom of the stairs.

Kevin had just come from the washroom on the bottom floor and saw this heap of humanity on the staircase. And like the rest of us, Kevin started laughing and could not stop. The event made for great retelling at Earls.

"It's a good job I didn't have to call 911 for you guys," Kevin told us. "I couldn't have done it. I was laughing too hard."

I have always felt it is important to end things on top. I never wanted golfers to walk by my table and say, "Oh, not Tait again." So, in the fall of 1994, I played my last hole at the country club. Keith Allen worked in the pro shop and had a great line when I putted out that day: "Cam, I guess you are now joining the senior tour."

Probably not. I'm content to look back with pride and satisfaction at my golfing career. Over three summers, we were at many tournaments, including Ronald McDonald House, the Craig Simpson Golf Classic, the Boys and Girls Club of Edmonton, Brooks Minor Sports, Viking Minor Sports, Alberta Easter Seals, the Canadian Paraplegic Association and others. Golfers from those tournaments, and others, contributed over $80,000. Thanks, folks, for the donations and the memories.

● ● ●

Now, back to No. 99.

It was Christmas Eve 1987 at Kevin Lowe's annual gathering when I knew Wayne had met the love of his life and future wife, Janet Jones. The ladies were upstairs, the men were downstairs.

"Well, guys, I think I am in love," Wayne announced. "I was with Janet last night and we went to the ballet. I really don't like the ballet, but when you are with the right girl, who cares, right?"

Wayne and I kept seeing each other after Oilers games. But I perhaps fumbled a rather big story.

Wayne was out with an injury in early 1988. When I interviewed him between periods as he sat out, he seemed a little more nervous than other times we had been together, but I didn't think it was much of a big deal. I thought I had a fairly decent story, but when I got to the *Journal* newsroom the next morning, my desk mate, Al Turner, met me with a frown on his face.

"I read that story you wrote on Gretzky this morning," Al said with a tinge of disdain in his voice. "Were you with him or did you do it over the phone?"

I told Al I was with Wayne.

"And he didn't tell you?"

"Tell me what?" I asked.

"CHED Radio ran with a story all morning. Gretzky and Janet Jones got engaged last night at Earls. You were with the guy and there was nothing in your story about him getting engaged?"

I began feeling beads of sweat on my forehead. It was a huge story in Edmonton. Wayne was like a prodigal son, and maybe I blew it.

"You didn't ask him?" Al said.

No, I replied, because I didn't hear anything to ask the question. Maybe Wayne wasn't sure what Janet's answer would be, so he kept quiet. Whatever the reason, I'd been scooped. In the news business, there's no feeling worse than that.

The Gretzky trade to Los Angeles forced a huge adjustment by the city of Edmonton and its hockey fans, but that first trip to Los Angeles to watch him play as a King showed me that they weren't the only ones. The kid from Brantford, who'd arrived in Edmonton all pimply-faced, long-haired and seventeen, was now an off-ice celebrity as well as a hockey superstar. In what amounted to a post-game dressing room party, there he was, swapping quips with people like actors Kurt Russell and Goldie Hawn, golfer Craig Stadler and syndicated radio host Rick Dees.

But the Gretzky bedrock was still solid. I'd made the trip to LA with my childhood friend, Barth Bradley, whom I'd managed to get into the dressing room with me. After we did the interview about the need for bone marrow, Wayne offered us a beer. We

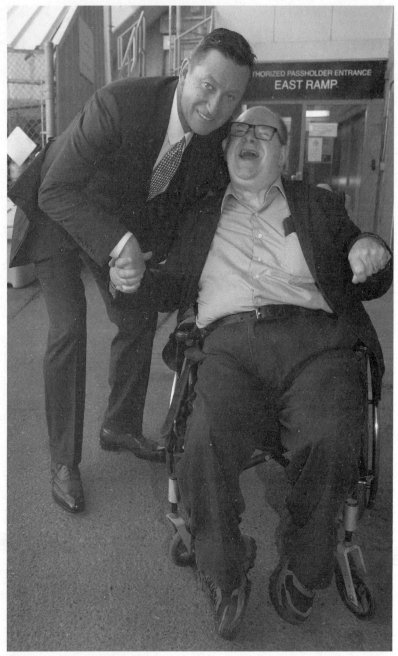

We were a lot older in 2014 when the '84 Oilers held their reunion, but for all of us, including Wayne Gretzky, the memories were as fresh as yesterday.

gratefully accepted, but didn't have a straw. Wayne got up from his stall, walked away from the reporters waiting to interview him and went scouring the Kings' dressing room before returning with two straws in his hand.

"I looked all over for these," he said.

"I know. I am pretty thirsty by now," I said, and heard the familiar Gretzky yowl.

One of the most amazing things about Wayne is how he always encourages people to look to the future. Whenever we had a chat at the morning skate of a game, he would end by saying, "You're coming to the game tonight, right? I'll see you after the game." And he would. It wouldn't be for very long because he had a plane to catch. But right before he left the rink, he would always say, "I'll find you when we are in town next." And he always did. His time was so restricted he often did not have time for more than a quick handshake and hello. But he always did that.

On my bookshelf there is a copy of *Gretzky! From the Backyard Rink to the Stanley Cup*, written by Jim Taylor with Wayne's dad, Walter. When I asked Wayne to sign it, he thought for a second, then wrote something I will always treasure: "To Cam. Thanks for all the fun times. Your friend, Wayne."

Right back atcha, 99. Right back atcha.

22

"C'mon Cam. I Dare You"

I was sitting in the front seat of a motorboat when I got a gentle elbow in the rib cage.

"Come on," Kevin Lowe said. "I dare you."

At that moment, cruising on the waters of Lake Shuswap in central British Columbia, I knew I had to go parasailing. I could not pass up a chance to parasail, never mind a dare from Kevin.

He sped up his boat to catch up to the boat that was advertising parasailing. Kevin flagged them down and shut the motor off.

"I think I have a customer for you," Kevin said, and then explained my disability to the driver.

"No problem," the gentleman said. "When do you want to go?"

We met in front of Kevin's cabin and got strapped in. Kevin and his brother-in-law, Bruce, put a special life jacket on me and put me in the water with the big sail behind me.

"We'll drag you behind the boat for a while, but when the wind hits the sails, you will go up," Kevin said before breaking into his great smile. "You're paid up in your life insurance, aren't you?

I laughed. "Sure am. But what a hell of a way to go."

Kevin told me his boat would be right beside the towboat.

"If you are in trouble and need to come down, raise your right hand and we will get you down," Kevin said.

I gave him the thumbs up and we were ready to go.

Giggling all the way up, once I was in the air I could stretch my legs and did not have to worry about sitting. It was an absolutely wonderful feeling of freedom. I found myself crying, not out of a sense of fear; they were tears of pure joy, thinking of all the people in my life who had encouraged and empowered me to do so many things, including those two friends below with their four kids, and Karen with her camera going full-tilt to record the moment.

The driver slowed the boat down and I thought the ride was over. But just when my feet were touching the top of the water,

There may be simpler ways to get a break from sitting in a wheelchair, but none more exciting than parasailing, as I did in 2003. PHOTO BY DEVYNS COVE

he gunned the motor again—and up I went. That must have happened four or five times before my adventure ended. When it did, I landed safely in the water. Kevin and Bruce were right there to lift me into their boat.

"Now you have something to tell your grandson," Kevin said.

"You better tell him," I suggested. "He probably wouldn't believe me."

The parasailing trip was just part of a magical weekend in 2003 at Kevin and Karen's, just north of Salmon Arm—and much of it involved his two boats.

I love sitting in a motorboat and whizzing down the lake, something I learned to enjoy while holidaying in Meota. But as I got older and heavier, we almost needed a crane to get me into a boat. Kevin, however, didn't see things that way. Joan and I arrived at the Lowes' one Friday afternoon and I was thrilled to sit on the deck overlooking the lake. The house and deck are above the beach, with steps made out of stone leading to the water. The thought of going down to the beach didn't even cross my mind, but Kevin had other plans. "Got any swim trunks?" he asked. "We're going boating."

"But how am I going to get down?" I asked.

Kevin stared at me. "You're with me. I am going to haul you down in your chair," he said. "Need any help getting changed?"

So off we went, Kevin tipping me in my chair and slowly guiding me thirty-seven steps down to the beach. When we got there, I was just going to relax and enjoy myself on the beach. Then Kevin brought a life jacket, put it on me, wheeled me down to the pier and helped lift me into the boat.

I was thrilled. "I can sleep here for the weekend," I said.

We went for a few laps around the lake and took the kids—Devyn, Keegan, Darby and Carly—water skiing. We turned off the motor in the middle of the lake, where Kevin reached into the cooler for some ice-cold beer. Halfway through them he helped me into the driver's seat and took my beer.

"No drinking and driving," he said. "Let's see how you do."

Kevin told me later that he knew I could turn the steering wheel myself. His only concern was how I would handle the throttle. I guess I passed the test, because after circling the lake a few times he told me to drive over to where his kids were swimming. Then he told them to get on their tubes and hang on to the rope.

"Hit it," Kevin told me.

I powered up and started to pull the kids in their tubes, overwhelmed and hardly believing what I was doing. The trust Kevin gave me, letting me not only drive the boat but trusting my abilities to pull all of his kids, is an experience I will never forget.

We spent another half hour on the water before we went in for dinner. As we were coming into shore, Kevin tapped me on the shoulder and pointed right in front of us.

"Cam, your cab is here," he said.

Kevin's father-in-law, Jerry Percy, had driven a bobcat down to the beach to get me back up to the house. Mr. Percy had chains to secure my wheels on the bobcat's front-end loader. He then lifted the loader and we roared up the hill to the house.

We flew back to Edmonton on the Sunday afternoon. A few hours before we left the lake, Kevin offered to help me have a sauna. I looked at the size of the narrow door and shook my head.

"C'mon, what are you saying?" he asked. "You go parasailing but you won't have a sauna on solid ground? Remember, you're with me."

And since I met Kevin in 1979, he has never let me down.

We met when the Edmonton Oilers joined the National Hockey League. When I visited the dressing room after practices or games, Kevin always said hello and shared extra time with me. He started a Christmas Eve tradition and had the team and several friends over at his home in South Edmonton. I was fortunate enough to be invited, along with Mom and Dad.

Our friendship really took off in 1985. I was covering charitable events for the *Journal*, including the Christmas Bureau, an agency that provides a festive meal to less fortunate people in Edmonton. Kevin loves Christmas and was the honorary chair. He arranged a Christmas carol singalong in the Rose and Crown, a popular downtown pub, to raise funds for the Bureau, and invited me to join him in a duet—"Frosty the Snowman"—his favourite. We never signed any recording contracts, but we had fun, and most importantly, raised some cash for the Christmas Bureau.

When I interviewed him, it was with my trusty notepad and pen, using the shorthand I had developed. Kevin said after he read a few stories and saw that all the quotes were right, he always felt comfortable with my interviewing technique.

Kevin moved into a new house with stairs. Lots of stairs. Whenever I arrived in a cab or with a friend, he would be the first to organize four or five guys to help me up the stairs. He took the back of my wheelchair and gave instructions to everyone as we went up. The same thing happened when we were going down. I always felt safe with Kevin. Always.

In 2006, he gave me the trip of a lifetime. He recalled me saying that I would love to go back to Philadelphia to visit The Institutes, so he arranged for me to travel on the Edmonton Oilers' charter. I really wanted to take my dad, but he wasn't able to go because of health issues. My friend Mark Scholz went with me to give me a hand. We toured the facilities and had a great visit with Glenn Doman, the man who developed the patterning program.

Kevin has been such a great friend. On the day my mother died, he called and asked me to dinner at his house and wanted me to stay the evening. In the winter of 2002, when he and Wayne were part of Team Canada at the Salt Lake Winter Olympics, Kevin had me phone him before every hockey game Canada played. The night before the Canada–USA gold medal game, I made my call. Kevin took it and said someone wanted to say hello.

One of Wayne's special friends is Joey Moss, who has Down syndrome and can be difficult to understand at times.

Kevin handed Wayne his cellphone.

"Hi Gretz. How are you?" I asked when I recognized his voice.

"Joey!" Wayne exclaimed, thinking I was Moss. "How nice of you to call."

And, he was serious.

"Sorry, Gretz. It's Tait."

There was a long pause at the end.

"Well, you've been drinking, haven't you? Have one for me."

Amazing, isn't it, how the years go by? I met the two of them as Oilers' players. Now they were both retired, Wayne out of hockey for now at least, Kevin struggling to rebuild the team as its president. Friendships, though, are ageless. It's one of the things that makes them wonderful.

23

Sit-Down Comedy

A mateur night at a stand-up comedy club. Of *course* I wanted to enter. What could possibly go wrong?

Okay, I couldn't stand up, my enunciation was iffy so people might not understand what I was saying, which would kind of take the edge off the punchlines, and I might get booed off the stage. But what else?

Well, one thing. As my friend Keith Thompson wheeled me up onto the stage to warm, if somewhat quizzical, applause, one raucous voice roared from the back of the room: *"Get that fucking cripple off the stage!"*

The room went dead silent. The tension in the crowd was palpable. I wanted to crawl into a cubbyhole. My *mom* was sitting right there with my dad, supporting me despite her dislike of the whole idea. She *heard* that.

But Keith was up to it. We'd worked up a five-minute routine, him doing some magic tricks and playing straight man. Ignoring the asshole, he swung right into it.

"Good evening. Cam and I are going to tell a few jokes," he

began. "But Cam does speak a little differently. Say, Cam, I have never asked you. Why do you talk funny?"

"I'm from Quebec," I answered. It brought the house down.

We were off and running, Keith asking questions about my disability, me keeping my answers as short as I could to help the audience understand me.

"I understand you have cerebral palsy, or as you call it, CP. Didn't you tell me your dad was very happy when the doctor told him you had CP?"

"Yes. He was very happy."

"How come?"

"He thought he had inherited Canadian Pacific."

The night continued with such nonsense. But the crowd kept laughing, which was music to our ears. But it wasn't unanimous. I looked over at Mom. The frown said it all. And how was I going to get around that?

I knew her feelings going in. She was not at all happy that I was going onstage, in a bar, to tell jokes about my disability. The idea had been the subject of much debate over several dinnertimes. I tried to make her understand that I wasn't laughing *at* my cerebral palsy, I was laughing *with* it. That's a huge difference. It was 1981, official International Year of Disabled Persons, where one of the aims was to show the able-bodied what we could do and how we could be an integral part of any community. What better way for me to do my part than to go up on that stage and take the laughs and the lumps with everyone else?

Although she would never admit it openly, I think Mom felt responsible for my birth and my problems because she was my mother. I have never felt that way—ever. To me, it was just one of those things in life that happened, and we managed to carry on quite well. Maybe that was part of the reason she just wasn't buying the stand-up idea. Truthfully, she wasn't alone.

My friend Rob Christie, the afternoon drive announcer on

630 CHED radio and the emcee of the event, had grave doubts about the audience being able to understand me, and seriously whether putting someone with a disability in a comedy contest was very cool. But he went along with the plan, and came through for us in great style at showtime with a really nice introduction as Keith wheeled me onstage—valuable seconds I needed to get over being scared stiff and quit asking myself what the hell I was doing there.

We got through it and had a great time. We didn't get the winners' trip to Los Angeles and the chance to work with professional comics in a club there, but the experience was enough to convince me that in the future there might be an opportunity for me to explore live comedy. I mean (*kaboom!*) dead comedy wasn't an option. Thank ya'. Thank ya' very much…

So, why would I try something like that? My answer to "Why?" has never changed: "Why not?"

People with disabilities *have to* stretch themselves, to move as much as possible into the mainstream with everyone else. Nobody's saying be stupid about it. I'm not going to attempt a pas de deux anytime soon, but that doesn't mean I can't enjoy ballet. Staying in the background, limiting yourself *because* of your disability, only serves to enforce belief among persons who are able-bodied that it's where you belong.

Rick Hansen was asked once about the difference between disabled and handicapped. "My *disability*," he said, "is that I can't use my legs. My *handicap* is your perception of that—and thus, of me." And then he wheeled around the world.

Comedians always intrigued me as a kid. More importantly, they gave me something to aim for. When I was a teenager, Jerry Lewis had a variety television show every week on CTV. I faithfully watched it and marvelled at how he could tell jokes and make people laugh. When I was in junior high school, Mom gained confidence in me and left me at home for a half hour or so. With nobody in the house, I'd grab a pen or a drumstick as my microphone and start telling stories as though I was doing my own show. And somehow, the jokes just poured out.

I never told anyone about my secret ambition to become an entertainer. They would have laughed, not at my material but at the loftily unrealistic goal, given my speech patterns and the way, many times, I could be difficult to understand. It was a private dream, a someday kind of thing. No sense giving them reason to mock.

The launch pad came from an unlikely source—my fellow students. Because I had written a few things, they voted to make me class valedictorian at our Grade 12 graduation ceremony. It was humbling, and downright scary. The speech I could do, but what if people didn't understand me? So, we coppered our bets, distributing copies of my speech to everyone at the grad dinner so they could follow along as I read.

Looking back now, we really didn't have to do that—and it would never be done today. But it got my foot in the door, and I remember the great feeling of being in front of a crowd and seeing them respond. I will always be grateful for the opportunity.

One thing I've learned about opportunities: when they come, you have to grab on with both hands. In 1992, I covered the Rainbow Society of Alberta, which helps fund dream trips for families with sick or disabled kids. One of their big fundraising events of the year was a media talent (no, that is not an oxymoron) show, which was started by radio announcer Don Percy when he was in Edmonton. But there was a problem. A month or so before the event, which I'd covered for several years for the *Journal*, Rainbow Society executive director Sandy Strogyn was on the phone, concern in her voice. There were only three acts for the talent night. In a leap of faith, I asked if I could try my hand at a comedy act.

"Are you sure you want to do this?" Sandy asked.

Yes, I was. And it forced me to sit down and write my own jokes. I knew if I went into a two- or three-minute bit, I would lose the audience because of my speech pattern. I set myself a four-sentence limit. If I could get to the punchline in the third sentence, even better.

My opening line was refined to "You may wonder why I talk funny. I'm from Calgary." A no-brainer. Edmonton and Calgary people grow up sneering at each other. My material must have worked, because I ended up winning the contest. But the big break came three years later.

Bill Medak had just taken over as general manager at the Yuk Yuk's comedy club at West Edmonton Mall. "I heard you speak at that golf tournament in Moose Jaw," he said. "You made me laugh. Why don't you come down to amateur night and see how you do."

If I could have, I would have jumped up and hugged Bill.

I started writing more and more material. I didn't know how long I was going to be onstage but wanted to be ready. I got there extra early to get my feet on the ground and met Ken Valgardson, a science teacher who hosted the show.

He'd read my work in the *Journal*, but he had his doubts.

"I know you can write," he said. "But I'm not sure about this. People in the audience can be very cruel."

I didn't bother mentioning that it was a song I'd heard before. (*"Get that fucking cripple off the stage!"*)

"All I want is a chance," I said.

"Okay. But don't say I didn't warn you."

I had great support from my friends. In fact, word swirled around the newsroom and several people from work came, including *Journal* photographer Greg Southam. Dad showed up with Bill Parenica, a gentleman he worked with. But Mom? Not a chance.

As Ken warmed up the crowd, I was even more motivated to do well. When you hear over and over again that you can't do something, you either shy away or your pride takes over and you find a way to get it done. I also had a secret source of motivation. I had a date that night—Tamara Kerrison—whom I had met the night I ran into Bill from Yuk Yuk's. I wanted to make a good impression on several levels. Dammit, I *would!*

There were three steps to get up to the stage. Ken introduced me and three of the waiters lifted me up and, as I would experience countless times in the future, I felt the momentary uneasy hush at the sight of the wheelchair, in some ways a sense of helplessness—wanting to lend a hand, but not knowing how.

For me, the challenge just compounds itself—and I welcome that. I know, damn well, if I do not come out with a great opening line, I am going to lose the audience forever.

I gave them the Calgary line. Comedy is like newspaper writing: If you don't get them in the lead, you're not gonna get them at all.

Big, big laugh. Some people even clapped. Okay, hit 'em again.

"When I was born, I didn't breathe for eighteen minutes. I have cerebral palsy. But, boy… did I ever get rid of the hiccups."

And:

"I went out and had a few beers when I turned eighteen, and I found out something very interesting. When I drink too much, I can walk a straight line."

And:

"I went to my banker the other day and he asked me if I would like some more overdraft. I said, 'Sure, I love every kind of beer.'"

And:

"I have a new job. I am an encyclopedia salesman and make eight thousand dollars an hour. It's easy—I say either you buy a set, or I will read it to you."

My five minutes flew by. Time to say goodbye…

"Have another drink. Have another eight drinks. It's all good. I am your designated driver."

I wheeled to the steps of the stage to warm applause. Some people were even standing as they applauded.

"Good job," Ken said as he shook my hand. Then, the words every comic lives to hear: "You had 'em. You really had 'em."

The first person I went to see was Dad. He didn't say a word, just put a hand on my shoulder. After the show was over, I asked Tamara if she wanted to go for a nightcap in a nice quiet lounge. She said yes. And just when I didn't think my night could get any better, the club manager asked me if I could come back the very next night and perform for five minutes before the professionals hit the stage. For a guy who couldn't walk, I seemed to be taking a lot of steps.

Now the work started. Anyone who thinks stand-up comedy is spontaneous obviously hasn't tried it. I haunted Yuk Yuk's every Wednesday to watch and learn and to try out new material. Ken Valgardson was a wonderful mentor, as was Rick Bronson, a seasoned veteran and funny man who often was the headline act at Yuk Yuk's. They drilled me on the mechanics of being onstage— when to move, how and where to move and, most importantly, the fundamentals of any appearance: work on a good, solid five minutes of material and then, little by little, add to it. I honestly think I inherited some of Dad's musical talents, especially with timing. I began realizing when to insert long pauses, when to speed things up and how to read a crowd. *Journal* managing editor Michael Cooke was also a big help, asking me to write a first-person piece about doing comedy, which ran on the front page. That wasn't just encouraging. It also brought some more people to Yuk Yuk's to see me.

The learning process was something akin to studying all week, then taking a Wednesday night oral exam. I was a little worried that I might need new material for every show. Then I realized that musicians don't write new songs for every show; they play their old favourites, the ones they know the people enjoy, and add new ones bit by bit. My situation, though, was a bit different. Being new to the game, I didn't *have* a big backlog. Time to start building one.

David Letterman has always been a favourite of mine. Christmas 1994 was approaching, so I stole the concept of Letterman's Top 10 list and came up with Tait's Eight, which I introduced at the end of my set.

Eight things I have never received for Christmas:

8. A pair of skis
7. Paint by numbers
6. A jigsaw puzzle
5. An Etch-a-Sketch
4. Needlepoint
3. Ski-Doo goggles
2. Skates
1. A chainsaw

I was encouraged by the audience's reaction to Tait's Eight, especially the Christmas list. Nobody came up to me after a show to say they had wished I could get those gifts. Instead, they said they could just visualize it in their mind's eye and it gave them a chuckle. I told Mom before that first-ever show that I wasn't laughing at, I was laughing with, and now the audience was doing the same thing with me. In the battle for acceptance and awareness of people with disabilities, I saw that as a wheel forward.

And, suddenly, there were road trips. Not just drive-to-the-next-town, drive-home, fall-into-bed-at-some-ungodly-hour. Actual *tours*, with all the disability glitches that implies.

In early February 1995, Rick was booked for two nights in Tantallon, Saskatchewan, near the border with Manitoba, and he asked if I was interested in coming along and opening for him. *Was I?* By then, thanks to his and Ken's generosity with gig times,

I had worked my way to anywhere from five to fifteen minutes. Now, a chance to test the act on the road? When do we leave?

Away we went, Rick and me along with my personal assistant, Taras Rawliuk. We travelled all night, arriving in Tantallon just before 3:00 a.m. There was a Pepsi-Cola sign right above the hotel door, so we called it The Pepsi Hotel. First clues that it wasn't the Ritz: No cars out front, just fourteen Ski-Doos, all in a row. No night clerk, just two room keys on the front desk. Two-storey building, no elevator. Hi, Cam. Welcome to show biz.

Rick and Taras helped me walk up the stairs and we entered my room with its red and white race-car wallpaper. Perfect! Washroom? Shared—and inaccessible. Couldn't even get my wheelchair through the door.

Taras managed to find a wash basin, so I stayed in my room all day with the fellows bringing food up to me. Let's just say I used the garbage can in my room in more ways than one that weekend and asked the hotel manager to make sure he gave it a good wash after we had left—or, better yet, throw it out.

I stumbled down the stairs an hour before the show and Rick told me I could do thirty minutes. It was a great opportunity for me to work on timing and new material. I think I did all right, because when I went off the stage people were standing and clapping. We repeated the routine the next day. Just as I was about to say goodnight, I called up the manager of the hotel to thank him, and to try a new joke.

"You have a great hotel here," I told him. "In fact, you do not have a five-star hotel—you have an eight-star hotel. I've never been in an eight-star hotel until I arrived this weekend. You see, there's a hole in the ceiling of my room, and at night, I can count eight stars."

Big laugh. It worked and I still use that line today.

I kept going to amateur nights faithfully, working on my

five minutes. I tried different words, different phrases, different timing to see how I could make it better. And I was getting into a new mindset in learning to spot potential material.

On a drive back from speaking to Ken's junior high school class in New Norway, a small town about an hour southeast of Edmonton, I noticed that Ken said "you know" quite a bit after he finished a sentence. Out of that observation came a new Tait's Eight list: Things that really sound a little strange with "you know" at the end.

8. The house is on fire, you know

7. Help! Help! Help, you know

6. The cheque is in the mail, you know

5. I want a divorce, you know

4. I'm in jail, you know

3. You know, you know

2. I'm pregnant, you know

1. I'm horny, you know

A few hours later at amateur night, it worked quite well. I was becoming more and more intrigued with the creative process and if I heard something that tugged at my brain, I tried to find a funny side to it. Then I couldn't wait until the following Wednesday to see if it worked or not.

Another thrill came in May, when I got a call from the Calgary Yuk Yuk's office telling me I would be the opening act for J.P. Mass in the Saskatchewan run. We performed in Moose Jaw, Prince Albert, Saskatoon and Regina, where I learned about the business on the road. I was paid $75 a night and Yuk Yuk's looked after the hotels and gas. I was responsible for food and spending money.

Comedy is a nighttime gig. To fill in the days, I arranged a series of interviews in advance, packed my laptop and wrote feature pieces for the *Journal*—which, lest we forget, was my day job and the way I was supporting my family while I chased this crazy dream.

Performing in Saskatoon was a treat. My brother, Brad, was in the audience and fifteen of my cousins made the two-hour drive from Meota to come see me, which meant a great deal. I did, however, miss Mother's Day because we were driving home from Regina. I called Mom to wish her a happy Mother's Day, which she appreciated. But she did not ask me about the tour. She was still not a big supporter of this comedy business.

The gigs kept coming: the British Columbia run with Rick, opening in Penticton, with stops in Kamloops, Vernon, Kelowna and Cranbrook, and a 30-minute spot headlining amateur night at the event where I'd gotten my start. This time it was in front of Dad, Joan and her entire family, friends like Wes Montgomery— Edmonton radio's legendary morning man, whose matchless stints as the master of ceremonies at various sports dinners helped keep my own comedic career dreams alive—oh, and lest we forget (he said snidely), a few people who'd said I wouldn't last.

Then, the big one, an amateur comedian contest at Yuk Yuk's involving comics from Edmonton and Calgary, the winner to represent Alberta at the national Yuk Yuk's Funniest New Comic showdown in Toronto.

Rick told me the rules of competition were very tight, especially when it came to time. Five minutes was all you had and if you went over, the judges were told to cut the microphone. Ever helpful, he arranged for extra spots for me so I could get tighter and tighter, and he monitored them with a stopwatch, shaking his head at my times: 7:15, 6:50 and 6:20. "Under five minutes or you'll be disqualified," he reminded me. "No second chances. Do five-oh-one, and you're gone."

So I rehearsed—in the shower, just before I went to sleep at night, in taxi cabs to and from assignments—anywhere that I could. I cut, sliced, hacked, found shorter words, anything and everything to get my set to five minutes, or even shorter.

The first night the round of competitors included seven or eight of the regular amateurs and three we hadn't seen before. I was fortunate enough to be in the top four to advance to the final night of the competition against another four from Calgary. In the week leading up to the big night, Rick worked tirelessly with me in person and by telephone, tightening the set even further. His mantra: "You can always get better." Lord, I hoped he was right.

I got to Yuk Yuk's a good two hours before showtime. The place was already half full. There was a real excitement in the air—another challenge I was ready to embrace. Mom and Dad were at the lake, and Dad wasn't sure he would make the five-hour drive for the show, but five minutes before the lights went down, I saw the doorman, Garth, usher him in along the far wall.

Okay! I was set. I felt this wonderful, unbelievable support from my family, right before I went onstage. That was all the motivation I needed.

All the comedians had great sets that night, a truly outstanding night of comedy. I was happy with my set, but didn't think it was the best. Well, I'd given it my best shot...

The judges tabulated their scores while the headliner entertained for a half hour, one of the longest thirty minutes of my life.

I knew I could have been better, but I felt I might be in the top three. Ken called up the third-place winner, who wasn't me. He called the runner-up, who wasn't me, either. Well, I'd tried...

Then I saw Garth casually walking by my table, trying not to look at me. Wait a minute! Garth and another young man always helped to take my chair up the steps to get me onstage. Why was he there now, unless...

Ken dragged out the suspense as he fumbled through his notes on stage.

"Our winner started coming to amateur night last November

It was a promotion shot for a comedy club appearance, so anything serious was out of the question. I think I managed that pretty well. Only a few people thought I'd finally cracked.

and I didn't really want to put him onstage because I didn't think anyone would be able to understand him," Ken told the crowd.

Just like that, Garth and his helper were hoisting my wheelchair. I was back up on the stage, not as a contestant, but as a winner. I looked out at Joan and she was crying. I asked Dad to come up and be recognized as the man who really taught me how to laugh. I felt a tremendous amount of achievement on several levels, the highest being that I had proved to myself and to the doubters that I could make people laugh. Sure, there'd be those who thought pity for my disability gave me an edge, but I didn't buy it. On that night, on that stage, I honestly felt it was because of my sense of humour.

When I came offstage, my good friend Bill Penny was at the side with a bottle of Sambuca.

"Open your mouth," he said, and poured in way too much. It set the tone for the night.

Two weeks later, we were off to the national finals at Yuk Yuk's in Toronto. I had few illusions about my chances. The competition would be top-notch and I was the only contestant from west of the Ontario border. So, view it as a trip, and enjoy the time.

I was right. I didn't win. But I had some fun. The Toronto Argonauts were really struggling that year, so I opened with, "You all think I'm here to do comedy. You're wrong. I am the new Argonaut starting quarterback."

• • •

I can be a very impatient person. It may help me in some situations, while in others, getting things done right away can be hurtful. Maybe I got too big for my britches. I thought because I did fairly well at Yuk Yuk's in Alberta, I would start to get regular work soon after the contest. That didn't happen and I was getting somewhat frustrated.

I had known entertainer Don Ast for a few years. He'd been one of the judges in 1992 when I performed at the Rainbow Society talent show, and he told me that if there was anything he could do to help, just call. So I did. I asked Don to act as my agent in an attempt to find me gigs. The only downside to that was I would be potentially ending my relationship with Yuk Yuk's because they did not deal with agents. All their bookings were done out of Calgary. It was a gamble, to be sure, but something I felt I had to do if I was going to get paid gigs. I kept going up on amateur nights at Yuk Yuk's but knew that could end anytime.

And it did. One of the toughest telephone calls I ever had to make was to Bill Medak, the general manager of Yuk Yuk's, and more importantly, the gentleman who'd opened the door for me. Bill had called me in early December to tell me he had a middle spot—fifteen minutes right before the headliner—for three nights in December. I had to call him back and turn it down because of my agreement with Don. It essentially ended my relationship with Yuk Yuk's. That was very hard for me to do because of the kind of man Bill is. All I could do was hope it would lead to better things.

24

You Can't Hurry Love

You think Errol Flynn was suave with the ladies? They had nothing on me. Consider my first date with the woman who would become my wife.

I had wanted to share my life with someone for years, but I approached the dating game like one of those TV show contestants who dress in ridiculous costumes and scream like banshees when their names are called. Strangely enough, it didn't work. And when it did, even on a single date, I'd fall hopelessly in love, push too hard too quickly and have my heart broken yet again.

I should have known better. My favourite music was Motown, and Diana Ross and the Supremes were my favourite group. And what was their big hit? "You Can't Hurry Love," which I'd heard and loved since I was seven years old. You'd think I'd have learned something from the title, let alone the lyrics. Not a chance.

Sure, I went to school dances, my folks driving me to and from. And I had dates. But somehow, even as an adult, I always had to drive the relationship at flank speed, and it never ended well. Halfway through a first-date dinner, I had plans for us for the next six or seven days. We would go to a movie, a hockey game, dinner with Mom and Dad, a walk in the park... because when I like something, I go after it.

On a first date I often had reservations at one of the best dining rooms in Edmonton, and if I really liked the woman, I sent her a bouquet of flowers the day before with the time I was meeting her written on the little card.

Romantic? Maybe. The kind of guy I am? Perhaps. Too much too soon? Oh yeah.

Take, for instance, a girl named Judy, whom I'd dated on and off for about ten months. Judy didn't mind picking me up in her little blue car and throwing my wheelchair into the trunk, which I truly appreciated. So, on her birthday, I said it was time she enjoyed the ride, told her to wear her best dress, picked her up in a stretch limousine, and had the driver turn into the drive-thru lane at McDonald's, lower the glass between us and ask, "Can I take your order, please?"

"A Coke, please," I said.

Judy didn't know whether to laugh, cry, or flee the car. She motioned that she didn't want anything. I asked the driver to park the limo so I could enjoy my Coke. Then we went to one of the most romantic dining rooms overlooking Edmonton.

Was I lonely? Perhaps. Did I want a meaningful relationship? Absolutely. But it didn't work. I was told over and over again that I was moving too fast. I've lost count of the times I heard, "I don't want to see you anymore," or "Cam, you're a great guy but I think we'd better just be friends." It hurt like hell. I was a little confused, too. People were telling me I was a good guy and had overcome so much. If I was so good, why didn't anyone want me as a boyfriend?

You see, I just didn't get it. In my youth I thought it was very important to get married young. That way, I thought, I wouldn't have to live in a nursing home, not if I had a wife to help me. I wasn't thinking of a young bride who had education, career and family dreams. I was just thinking about how I wanted someone to cook, clean and help me get dressed, and when I had an accident in the washroom, she wouldn't mind cleaning it up… would she?

I will never forget the wise words Gary McPherson once shared with me over a Scotch when one of us was broken-hearted from a fresh romance: "It takes a very special lady to wipe your ass when you're on the can, and then, an hour later, make love to you."

That's when the loneliness set in, and with it, a sense of isolation. Fortunately, in the spring of 1995, I decided on one last kick at the cat. I asked my roommate, Taras Rawliuk, if any of his girlfriend's friends might be interested in meeting me. He made a few calls and set up a date on my mother's birthday, April 21, at West Edmonton Mall. My dad dropped me off and I saw this vibrant woman in a pink top and jeans walking toward me.

I knew there was something special about this Joan Bianchini. The way she smiled said it all. We had a drink in a lounge in the mall and then I suggested we go to Yuk Yuk's comedy club. Okay, I left out one tiny detail: I didn't tell Joan I'd be onstage that night telling jokes.

Ten minutes before I went onstage, I excused myself to use the washroom. The next time Joan saw me, I was behind the microphone doing my thing. I finished and went back to the table.

"Come here often?" I asked.

We started seeing each other and I quickly found out what a caring person she is. Joan is the oldest of thirteen children and grew up in Edmonton. When I met her, her son Darren was 24 years old. I knew I was in love when she brought a bottle of wine over to my house and we sat on the couch watching *The Lion King*.

Joan just made me feel so comfortable to be with. She is nine years older than me and was keeping me grounded. I decided one afternoon at work to propose to her that night, six weeks after we had met. I didn't have a ring, but that didn't discourage me at all.

Joan was working noon to 8:00 p.m. as a credit specialist with GE Capital. We met at the Edmonton Country Club for a drink about 9:30. It was a lovely warm evening. Before we went into the clubhouse, I asked her to sit on the bench by the first tee.

"This is where it all begins," I said, pointing to the first tee. "Joan, I love you and want you to be my wife."

I took off my watch. "I don't have a ring, but I want to give you my time—the rest of my life. Will you marry me?"

She looked down for a few seconds, which seemed an eternity, then lifted her head. There were tears in her eyes. She nodded and said yes.

The next day we went to tell Mom and Dad, who stood up and hugged us both. That was a very special moment for me, to see how happy my parents were. We then shared the news with Darren and the rest of Joan's family. Then it was off to my friend Tom Towns' jewellery store to buy a ring. It was official.

Joan and Darren moved in with me in my house over the summer. I always said I would never live with someone until I was married, but I wanted to be with her all the time. And, in what seemed like moments later, there I was, looking down the very long aisle of St. Joseph's Basilica, thinking I must be dreaming. Because there she was, in a red wedding dress and matching hat, walking toward me to become my wife. The church was packed with more than five hundred relatives and friends, but I didn't see them. Only her, my darling Joan.

We were married on November 11 to honour the memory of Joan's parents, who both were in World War II and have passed away. We got married in the evening and gathered to have pictures taken at a downtown hotel. I could not believe how beautiful Joan looked. It took my breath away.

The reception was held at the Edmonton Country Club. I

Sometimes, you just get out-of-this-world lucky. In the spring of 1995, a friend set me up on a blind date with a woman named Joan Bianchini. Six weeks later, I proposed. The Oilers should be that lucky when they draft.

surprised Joan by singing a duet with my friend Muriel Scott: "Have I Told You Lately That I Love You?" (Yes, I have been known to sing in places other than the shower. When I took that trip to Toronto for the Yuk Yuk's finals, Joan came with me, despite her lifelong discomfort over flying. To take her mind off the fact that we were hurling through the air, I stroked her back and sang the Mickey Mouse song to her. Eat your heart out, Errol.)

I thought I knew what it meant to have a great family, as I'd had with my mother and father. But when I married Joan, my understanding of having a family rose to a whole new level. At the reception, I tried to put it into words.

"Joan," I told the reception crowd. "Thank you for giving me the son I never had."

Darren came up to the microphone and we embraced in a hug. It was a tender moment for almost everyone in the crowd, and that gave me a chance to change the tempo.

"Now," I told him, "go get me a drink."

• • •

In 1997, Joan and I moved into a condo in south Edmonton—brand new. In fact, we had our unit designed with wider doorways and a wheel-in shower. But the real selling point was the 24-hour home care we have in the building. Seven of us with physical disabilities moved into the condo complex and pooled our home care funding to hire personal care attendants. It has made Joan and me more independent of each other.

My mother said my life would change the day I was married, and she was absolutely right. I now had a reason to come home from work—a wife and stepson. It took me several years to fully embrace being a family man, and part of that was a huge mind shift for me. All my life I had been told that I had to be taken care of; that people had to help me; that my needs came first. And when you're constantly in that environment, it's hard to think of yourself as someone who can care for others.

That all changed on December 22, 2002. Just after 5:00 p.m., Joan zoomed around the corner of a maternity ward at the Misericordia Hospital.

"It's a boy. It's a boy," she beamed as she spread the news of our brand new grandson: Nicholas Jordan Davis. What made it even sweeter was that he was born on the same day as my father. A great Christmas gift.

Over the next few months, we became very comfortable with Nicholas. Darren and his wife, AnnaMai, moved within five minutes of our place. When AnnaMai went back to her work for the Province of Alberta, Joan babysat Nicholas every weekday. I was working for the *Journal* from home by then and it was a real treat for me.

My time with Nicholas when he was small was so priceless. When I heard Darren unlock the door just after seven on weekday mornings to drop him off, my day as a father and grandfather only got better. Darren would lay Nicholas in our bed, between Joan and me. We would sleep for another hour before waking up and starting our day together. I do not have a lot of control in my arms, so picking Nicholas up and holding him would be too dangerous. So, we improvised. When Joan took her morning shower, she put Nicholas safely on the couch and I wheeled up beside him and made sure he didn't fall off.

I really saw how caring Joan is with Nic. But she gave us a terrible scare one afternoon when she was lying down on the bed. One of my personal care attendants was in our condo and, in a panic, said she needed to call 911. I thought Nic had fallen. But, no. Joan was complaining of chest pains. One of the most poignant pictures I ever saw was Nic following the stretcher as Joan was being wheeled down the hallway into an ambulance, saying, "Nana, don't go."

Joan had a minor heart attack and was in the hospital for a week or so. It was a good reminder for us to slow down.

We are a team. We have our disagreements and heated discussions, like any married couple. But she has taught me so much and I know I am a much better person—especially in my spending.

Joan said she married me because I made her laugh. She does the same for me. A year after we were married, she made chocolate pudding for dinner. I love chocolate pudding but I tend to get it all over myself—especially that night.

"We don't need any kids," Joan said, surveying my mess. "We have you."

Ah, Diana, you were Supremely correct. You can't hurry love. But when you do find the right one, the wait is worth it.

It's amazing how attached I became to our grandson. Since I never had children of my own, I didn't know what to expect. But Nic and I formed a special bond. Maybe we had to. His mother, and our daughter-in-law, AnnaMai, received some devastating news in 2007. She had advanced colon cancer and was given twenty-one months to live. Doctors couldn't do anything.

AnnaMai, who was born in the Philippines, was a fighter. She took chemotherapy and I was so proud of the way she and Darren dealt with her treatments. They made it a family day: Darren took the day off work, Nic was taken out of school, and Joan and I shared the day with them.

For five years AnnaMai fought the disease to a standstill, and even showed some improvement. But cancer is so lethal. Both Joan and I could see that she was getting weaker and enduring more pain. Joan took her to see her doctor on February 22, 2013. The doctor took one look at AnnaMai and called an ambulance. She fought going. All she wanted to do was go home and see Nic. But hospital was, however temporarily, the only answer.

Joan embraced taking care of Nic, and I tried to spend as much time as I could at the hospital with Darren. Three days after

AnnaMai went into the hospital, she slipped further. Shortly after four in the afternoon, the doctor met with Darren and me to tell us AnnaMai's kidneys had shut down. She had only days to live.

Darren knelt down beside her bed and, for the second time since I'd become his stepfather, cried in my lap. The first came in January 1996, when his father took his own life. And now, his beloved wife was slipping away. An hour later, I was sitting in the waiting room just outside AnnaMai's ward on the fifth floor. My heart was in my throat when I saw Nicholas in his very colourful ski jacket, skipping down the floor toward me. Darren wanted to take Nic for a walk himself to tell him the news.

"How's Mommy, Papa?" he asked with his typical enthusiasm.

"She's okay," I whispered, knowing full well she wasn't.

My heart broke for our family. Yet, Nicholas was so strong. Joan and I both commented on his attitude. I felt so bad for Darren, thinking of what was in front of him.

March 2 was a Saturday in 2013. Darren stayed at the hospital that night with AnnaMai's family. At 6:23 a.m., we received the call we dreaded: please bring Nic to the hospital to say goodbye to his mother. AnnaMai passed away within the following hour.

Nic found great comfort in hockey. He had a game the morning after his mom died. We wondered whether he should play, but he wanted to, and play he did, scoring two goals.

There was more. Right after the game, his novice team coach, Shaye Ganam, shut the dressing room door and asked Nic if he wanted to say anything. Shaye told us later that Nic stood up and said, "When you go home tonight, make sure you hug your mom. Because I don't have one anymore..."

Darren and Nic stayed at our condo for a week. We felt a real need to be together. Nic had his moments, but I was amazed at the way he kept talking about hockey. Several times a day, we went downstairs together in our underground parkade, where Nic shot hockey pucks against the wall. I will never forget him sitting cross-legged on the cement floor when he needed a rest. He talked about his mom and then talked hockey, saying that he wanted to be in the National Hockey League. And then he got up and shot twenty more pucks.

Yes, I am a grandfather. Yes, I dote on Nic. Time with him is magic, and when he scored his first goal, well...Gretzky who?

His strength amazed me, absolutely. And he kept getting stronger. AnnaMai's funeral was held at St. Joseph's Basilica, where Joan and I had been married. In Catholic tradition, the coffin is draped with a white baptismal cloth before the service. Nic and Darren spread the cloth with such care and tenderness, and it profoundly touched me. I was sobbing uncontrollably as I wheeled up the aisle with Darren, Nic and Joan.

After we reached the front row on the right side of the church, I buried my head in my hands and cried. All of a sudden I felt this little hand on my left shoulder.

"Papa," Nic said in a strong and reassuring voice. "Don't worry. Everything is going to be okay."

My 10-year-old grandson, who had just lost his mom, was comforting me. All I could do was hug him, and try to bottle up my tears. Because I knew he was right. We were a family. We had each other, and memories of AnnaMai to hold in our hearts forever.

Paying It Forward

Understand this: I refuse to be a poster boy—ever.

Shortly after I joined the *Journal* in 1985, I was asked to speak at an "awareness night" for a social-activist group which, in fairness, shall remain nameless. I spent a lot of time preparing a speech on my life's story. But I never got to use it: when I arrived at the venue, I introduced myself to the organizer and asked when I was speaking and for how long.

"Oh, we've decided not to have you speak," she said. "We just want you to sit on the stage so people can see you in your wheelchair."

I called a cab and got the hell out of there—angry, humiliated, insulted, but aware of a disturbing truth: there were people out there, well-meaning, good-hearted people organizing nights like the one I'd just left to help others—and they didn't have a clue. "Hey, we need to show we're about helping improve the lives of people with disabilities. Get me somebody in a wheelchair and stick him onstage!"

Who knows? Maybe it was the push I needed. Since that first night at Yuk Yuk's, I'd always had a feeling that there was something more meaningful I could do with my humour, something that could deliver a message along with the laughter. My brother Brad's wife, Kathy, had watched *100 For Cameron* over and over again and told me more than once that I should be spreading the word about the patterning program that had done so much to shape my life, because the story could be an inspiration for others facing the same situation.

I had never thought about doing that, because, for some reason, I had blocked a lot of what we did from my mind. I don't know why. Perhaps it was because I knew my family had given up so much to take the program on, and that made me uncomfortable. But as I thought more and more about it, I realized that Kathy was right. My childhood was a cornerstone of my life. And it wasn't just about what we did. It was the people and the wonderful community support we had. As a tribute to them, if nothing else, I needed to tell that story more than I had been.

The summer of 1997 was spent trying to get as much information as I could on what we did. My memory is quite good and is almost photographic, but I spent many afternoons with Mom and Dad and had them fill in the blanks.

At first, I struggled with finding the right way to map it out as a presentation. Maybe it was too close to me. But deadlines have always inspired and motivated me. So when the press release crossed my desk about the Rainbow Society media talent night, I knew I could do something different.

I have never spent much time rehearsing material. But with the Philadelphia story, I found myself rehearsing over and over again. I wanted to get it down just right.

Also, I'm seldom nervous before a performance. But the day of the Rainbow Society event, I was a mess. My friend Bill Penny dropped by with my favourite bottle of rum and wanted me to have a snort with him in the afternoon, which I politely declined. I knew this was an important story to share and I didn't want to mess it up. And that in itself told me I was zooming in on nailing it.

My theme was "freedom," and how my folks and all the volunteers gave me the freedom to do so much. It also gave me a chance to use the riveting quote from the Martin Luther King speech: "I have a dream." I decided to incorporate it into my presentation, and even had the audience repeat those four wonderful words. I sprinkled in a few of my favourite lines from the comedy routine to try to make it as entertaining, and yet as informative, as possible. I found this very challenging, but creative.

The presentation was very well received. The response from the audience was warm. I have learned to be able to read what crowds say. What they told me that night was that the story needed to be shared.

People were amazed to hear about the volunteers who helped us with patterns. Hearing the response, some four decades after we completed the program, made me ask a very daunting question: Would there be the same support from volunteers and neighbours if a child needed similar assistance in the late 1990s?

The potential answer—no—scared me. The world had so many new distractions and people were starting to work longer and harder hours. Technology was beginning to make talking in person and sharing time with one another a thing of the past. A piece in *National Survey on Giving and Volunteering* in the mid-1990s cemented my suspicions. People were not volunteering as they used to. There was an opportunity to encourage people to volunteer through telling my story. It was more than a project; it was a responsibility.

I changed the theme to "time" and thought of several four-letter words we use when we talk about time: I will *make* time for you; if I can *find* the time; I will *take* time for you; I have time to *kill.*

But there's a five-letter word that describes what we do very well with time—share. Because where do you make time—in the microwave? Where do you find time—behind Grandma's couch? Where do we take time from—the bottom kitchen drawer?

Of course not. We share time, and that is the greatest gift we give to each other. So, why do we minimize that? Why do we use words that can be viewed as a task about as comfortable as having a root canal?

Sure, times have changed in so many ways since we did patterns in the 1960s, but we should never, ever forget the importance of being with each other, of helping each other and celebrating each other. And, maybe, when we do that we are sharing ourselves with one another. I was extremely fortunate as a child to have many people share their time with me and to be hands-on in so many ways. Maybe my story could encourage more people to engage in community projects, to help others.

Perhaps because I wasn't able to play sports as a kid, I had time to watch and really study coaches. I began to admire what they do and had a particular fascination with how coaches motivated their players. I have always had a secret ambition to be a coach—to put people in environments, mentally and physically, to succeed to their full potential. Other than helping with that Little League team in 1979, I didn't have an opportunity to coach sports.

Here was my opportunity, with my speaking engagements, to tell my story. I know it will never meet the expectations of everyone in the audience. My aim is to reach one person in the crowd. I never know who that person is or how I might motivate them, if in fact I do. But that's the goal I set whenever I speak.

It's important, I think, not to speak at the audience, but to speak with them and try to always engage them. I kept the Martin Luther King reference and the "I have a dream" speech and had the audience repeat it after me. And I decided to spruce it up a little.

"Please repeat after me in memory of Martin Luther King," I said to the audience. "I have a dream today."

The audience repeats.

"To remember."

Audience repeats.

"To remember how to spell."

Audience repeats.

I pause for several seconds. Then: "Supercalafragalistic-expealadocious."

That usually gets a laugh and warms up the crowd to what we are trying to achieve.

"Okay, now we're warmed up. Let's do it again. I have a dream."

Audience repeats.

"And I owe it to myself to go get that dream."

I stressed the importance of having a dream and sharing it with people, who then became part of it.

Like any new project, it took time to get its legs. I must have sent out eight million emails to groups telling them about my speaking project, with very little response, but I couldn't give in to the lack of interest. I owed my volunteers so much more than that.

In the fall of 1998, I asked Anne Kirkpatrick if she would help me get the word out. Anne and I had met five years earlier when I was a loaned representative for the United Way. With her help, I sensed a new life in the project. She suggested showing a video. Don Metz of Aquila Productions staff suggested we produce a "now" and "then" video, using clips from the CBC documentary and shooting some new video of what my day now looked like.

My day started at 4:30 a.m. and Don said he would have a cameraman at my door at that time. Sure enough, cameraman Bryce York was knocking at my door five minutes early. I met him sitting in my chair, wearing only a towel. Fifteen years later, Bryce still tells the story and doubles over in laughter. Then a look of complete disgust washes over his face before he says, "It's a sight you do not want to see. Ever!" I think he could very well be right.

Bryce followed me around all day, to and from the *Journal*. The Toronto Maple Leafs were in town that night to play the Oilers. Bryce got some good footage of my dear friend Miles Pollak, who worked as the press box gate attendant at Oiler games, grabbing me under my left arm and helping me walk up the two flights to the press box at Rexall Place while my guest brought up my wheelchair. Post-game, we visited the Toronto dressing room. Curtis Joseph was with the Leafs then, and we exchanged a few giggles, which Bryce got on video.

The editors at Aquila then cut two three-minute segments, using Bryce's stuff and the CBC footage from 1966, plus video from my wedding shot by my old NAIT buddy, Ken Sellar. Don suggested I bookend the presentation with the videos. We titled the show *Freedom of Speech* and chose the song "Freedom" by the Pointer Sisters for the ending because, in many ways, I felt the work done by my folks and the volunteers helped give me freedom to give, love and dream.

Opening night! I knew now how they must feel on Broadway. This was my *Oklahoma*, my *Chicago* or *Cats*. Smaller numbers, of course. The Winspear Centre in downtown Edmonton sat 2,700 people, had three balconies, and acoustics so amazing that during sound check my voice could be heard in the top row even without the microphone we'd be using during the show for the Glenrose Foundation. The foundation is the fundraising arm of the Glenrose Rehabilitation Hospital, which does amazing work, helping people adjust to their new lives following a spinal cord injury, a stroke, a heart attack and so many other unfortunate health issues. This was launch night of its capital campaign. Among those who'd be in the audience were Dorothy and Allan Kissack, the couple who really helped get my patterning going in

1964, who were driving in from Lloydminster. No pressure, Cam, just be great.

Bruce Bowie, my closest friend in the Edmonton media, who was the morning man for CISN-FM, was the master of ceremonies. Bruce had a very personal connection with the Glenrose because his wife, Mary, had sustained a brain injury when she was hit by a vehicle while going for a walk one evening, and she went to the Glenrose for rehabilitation.

Drew Hutton of the Glenrose Foundation made sure Bruce and I were taken care of. We both had our own dressing room before the show. "We're already dressed, right?" I asked Bruce. "So why don't we just go in mine and visit?"

There are some people in my life that let me revert to being a kid when I am with them. Bruce is one of them. The washroom door in my dressing room opened out, so I started slamming it shut. The harder I slammed it, the more Bruce laughed. Truth be told, I was trying to see just how much force it would take before it would come off. Nervous much?

"You know, there's about fifteen hundred people getting into their seats right now to hear you speak," Bruce said as he looked at the clock. "And you're more worried about breaking the bathroom door?"

I smiled and gave it one more whack.

"Yep, you bet," I said.

Bruce and I share the Christian faith. I asked him to lead us in prayer, seeking for help from above. He did, and then, just like clockwork, Drew knocked on the door to lead us to the stage.

"I think I heard some banging," he said as he led us through the back halls of the Winspear.

"Banging?" I asked innocently. "I didn't hear any banging."

Bruce went out and welcomed the crowd before introducing a wonderful group of Japanese drummers. Then it was my turn.

It was May 19, and the premiere of the new Star Wars movie,

The Phantom Menace. Drew handed me a light sabre just before I went onstage. I wheeled out, backwards of course, waving the light sabre.

"This is the real premiere of Star Wars," I opened with.

After a laugh from the crowd, I asked everyone to think of the person they came to the Winspear with and to join hands with them. I then asked them to repeat after me the phrase, "Thank you for your time." On that cue, the folks in the production booth played the first bookend of the video.

I wheeled off to the side of the stage and, as the video played, I felt an incredible sense of accomplishment, of seeing a vision come to reality—in such an elegant venue as the Winspear.

The quality of the first video was great motivation for me. I knew I had to dig deep, and give everything I had to keep the momentum going. I simply wheeled back onto the stage and told my story. My voice did crack a little when I introduced Mom and Dad and my wife.

The ending of a presentation is critical. I think you have to leave the audience with a challenge—not only to help others, but themselves. After the second video, a white on black graphic appeared: WHAT IS YOUR FREEDOM?

My hope was that the audience would ask themselves what things in their lives gave them dignity and independence—and then challenge themselves to share that gift with others. We had the wonderful 1969 song "Get Together" by The Youngbloods playing as the music bed under the freedom graphic. I waved to the crowd, thanked them for their time and began wheeling off the stage. I managed to find Joan in the third row and she had that special look of pride that told me I did okay. The crowd was standing and the applause thundered. I didn't realize it at the time, but I was in the middle of one of the most magical nights of my life.

As I was heading back to my dressing room to give the

bathroom door one more slam, just for the hell of it, my long-time friend Bryn Griffiths met me in the hallway.

"Where do you think you're going?" he asked. "There's about a million people out there who want to shake your hand—and I'm one of them."

Bryn and I were chatting in the hallway when Father Mike McCaffrey showed up.

"How did you get back here?" I asked.

Mike looked at me with that smile he wore just before he gave a zinger. "I know the doorman, the Man Upstairs," he said. Then he bent down and whispered something in my ear that I will never forget.

"God is pretty proud of you tonight," he said.

We went out the door into the lobby. People were waiting to greet me with handshakes and hugs. I really don't think they were congratulating me for what I had just shared with them; rather, I felt they were celebrating the strength of a community coming together for a common need. And, hopefully, it made them look into their own lives and want to share their time with others.

It took me over thirty minutes to get through the lobby and the well-wishers—a very gratifying experience. Halfway through the crowd, I saw Dad holding court with five people listening to him talk. He was using a cane by then to help him with his balance. But that night, Dad was using his trusted cane as an exclamation point, raising it as far as he could for emphasis. I smiled widely to see my father enjoying such a wonderful night.

Joan and I went for a drink at the Chinese restaurant just down the street from our condo. It was the perfect way to cap off an unbelievable night.

26

Teach Your Children Well

During my reporting gig with *The Spokesman*, I went to Camrose—a small city an hour southeast of Edmonton—in 1980 to cover a 4-H conference. There were several speakers with disabilities and we thought it would make a good story.

An unexpected door opened when we arrived at the conference. They were short one speaker for one of the breakout sessions. The organizer knew I was there as a reporter, but asked if I would fill in. I jumped at the opportunity. We were given thirty minutes to talk about disabilities to twenty teenagers. Using some of my humour, to my great surprise, most of the kids laughed. That gave me a great deal of confidence that, just maybe, there was a future for me in public speaking.

My timing was good. The United Nations had declared 1981 International Year of Disabled Persons, and there were many initiatives in the world to create a better understanding about disability. A local theatre group, Catalyst Theatre, was planning to put on a play called *Creeps* in early January. *Creeps* is a powerful play written by Canadian playwright David Freeman.

The entire play takes place in the men's washroom in a sheltered workshop where men with disabilities vent their anger and frustration about how little society would let them fully participate. Jan Selman directed the play and made a few calls to Edmonton agencies that helped people with disabilities. I volunteered to work with the actors so they knew the characteristics of cerebral palsy.

I wonder, though, what they thought when they first met me. We met at two o'clock at *The Spokesman* office on December 10— my twenty-second birthday. A friend had invited me for lunch. We had a few beers and he gave me my birthday present, an oversized baseball cap with earflaps. On the earflaps, two words: "Bullshit Protector." Naturally, I had to wear my new cap back to work. (Okay, maybe we'd had a *lot* of beer.)

I wheeled backwards into the office, half-drunk, with my new cap and the flaps tied at the bottom. The four actors were sitting quietly in the reception area.

"Mr. Tait, your appointment is here," the receptionist said.

"Hello men," I said. "Come on in and I will show you how to act."

Those poor guys didn't know how to react. But we hit it off perfectly. They were very eager to learn what cerebral palsy was all about.

Three days before the show opened, Jan called to say she wanted to have a discussion on disability following every performance, and would I be interested in hosting several of them. Again, I jumped at the chance.

"But we do have one request, Cam," Jan said. "Please don't wear your birthday cap."

On opening night I had just returned to Edmonton by bus from North Battleford. I thought if I began with a joke, maybe it might relax the audience.

"I just got back from North Battleford on the Greyhound—not

the doggy. I went up to the driver and he looked at my ticket and made sure I was going to Edmonton. 'Hell no,' I told him. 'I am going to Vancouver. I'm your relief driver.'"

Creeps was a big success and the post-show talks went well. The exposure, coupled with the response to the Winspear Centre show, helped get the word out that I was on the public-speaking market. It got me several keynote gigs, some even paying as much as a thousand dollars. I asked Anne Kirkpatrick to handle the business side of things because I have always struggled with that. We were a great team. Amazingly, she insisted on doing it as a volunteer, even though I was being paid. She said she was just happy to see me living my dream.

We agreed that it was still important to provide the show for free when groups could not afford a speaker. Many of the requests we got came from charities that did not have the finances for my fee. I really thank Anne for keeping me grounded.

The following April was very busy for us. National Volunteer Week was the third week of the month and we made the presentation available to charities that wanted to thank volunteers, but also to encourage them to keep sharing their time. We made appearances all over the province and Anne drove me back and forth from Edmonton. I made sure all of her expenses were covered, and when we had a meal on the road, I paid the bill.

I had a big break in November 1998, when the Canadian Airlines Foundation flew my cousin Dave Tait and me to London, Ontario, to speak to a national youth conference on volunteerism. It was perhaps one of the few times when I was caught off guard onstage. When I asked the crowd to repeat the "I have a dream" line, one student in the front row repeated it all right—very loudly, exactly the way I talked. I was a little taken aback, but really couldn't blame the young man. He was doing exactly as I asked.

In the fall of 1999, Volunteer Canada, a national body that

promotes volunteerism, invited me to speak at a conference in Montreal, and what a whirlwind trip it was. I arrived late Friday afternoon and was met by a conference volunteer, who was also assigned to be my personal attendant.

The next morning, I was feeling motivated and energized to be on the road, sharing my story. The spirit of the conference was creating your own opportunities, so I decided to do just that.

Joan had bought me a brand new Gillette razor for the trip, and after my morning shower, I decided I would shave myself. I made sure I had extra lather on my face, you know, just in case... The first three swipes went great. But on the fourth I felt something cut. At first, I thought I was okay because I didn't see any blood. Then, I looked again, and it was pouring onto the floor from my right cheek.

Oops!

I grabbed as many towels as I could to wipe the white tiles on the bathroom floor. I then managed to stop the bleeding from my cheek before I called room service for a Band-Aid. The poor young woman who came to my room was in shock to see the bathroom floor, which was checkered with white towels covered in blood. It probably didn't help that it was Halloween morning.

After I got patched up, away I went to speak at the conference. I was asked to speak in a breakout session on the impact of volunteering. The total audience? Four. Yes, four people. And three of those four were from Edmonton, and had heard my presentation before. But what the heck. We were in Montreal and made the most of it. I flew back to Edmonton the next day and had some explaining to do when Joan met me at the airport and saw the cut on my cheek.

Not every engagement was as adventurous.

Slowly, we were getting requests from all kinds of groups, ranging from community leagues to a breakfast attended by Royal Bank senior managers.

For a while, I had a website, and the brochure certainly helped. But not as much as word of mouth, and I think that was perhaps our best way to promote the show. From my own experience, I remember the excitement and motivation I felt after attending a performance or speech that moved me—and I was trying to create that same kind of experience for my audiences.

I was getting more and more comfortable with the presentation. A big part of that was the response from the audience on the story of how our volunteers were so faithful. During the question-and-answer segment at one engagement, one woman stood up in the audience and said she was one of the people who had come into our home to help us. That was a very tender moment.

National Volunteer Week continued to be a busy time for us. In 2001, I had a speaking engagement every night of the week; in fact, I was invited to two different non-profit groups in Ponoka, Alberta, an hour south of Edmonton—one on Monday night, and the other on Thursday. It was heartwarming, yet a little alarming, to see several of the same volunteers at both events. I think that shows how many volunteers share their time with different agencies. And that same story is played out time and time again throughout Canada.

Sol Rolingher is a partner of the law firm Duncan and Craig in Edmonton and is very involved in the Edmonton community. When the firm celebrated its 100th anniversary in 1994, Sol spearheaded the Laurel Awards, which are cash prizes to three local charities for innovative programs. They asked me to be the keynote speaker at the 2001 awards luncheon, which was attended by government and business leaders. Sol made sure Mom and Dad were seated at a front table. I was thrilled whenever my parents were at a presentation so the audience could recognize them for being the true heroes they were. Dad loved it, but Mom—who was by nature very shy—found it to be uncomfortable. Yet, I felt they were role models and could shine a beacon of light for parents everywhere.

In 2001, Anne and her husband, Jeff, moved to Airdrie, Alberta. I felt a great sense of loss, because Anne was such a great proponent for the message I was trying to convey about volunteering, about treating one another with respect and kindness. On the business side of things, Anne was so professional—yet kind—and took care of the details so I could just focus on the onstage presentation. She had helped me to lay the foundation of the project and worked tirelessly to keep it growing. Now I was motivated to make it even better, as a kind of thank you to Anne.

I wanted to stress the commitment of our volunteers who kept coming back week after week to help us do patterns. I also began to appreciate that, even though my voice could be understood by most people, an hour or more might be asking a little too much. And it became increasingly evident that everyone was being asked to do more and more and the time we had for ourselves and others was becoming less and less.

So I went back to Don Metz with a new idea for the video: have a digital clock, starting at 00:00 and run it right through to 60:00 for an hour presentation. I wanted to give the audience just a little sense of urgency, that when the clock ended, it was time to go out and help their community.

"I have one of my best editors returning Monday from holidays," he deadpanned. "He will be so excited when I tell him we have an hour-long piece to cut of nothing but a clock running. He's going to love me."

But then I made it interesting. Since every pattern was five minutes, I asked him to stop the clock every five minutes and insert thirty seconds of video from the CBC documentary of a patterning being done, then start the digital clock where it left off. I wanted to show the audience that in sharing five minutes, they can make significant changes to somebody's life. I was just one example.

Broadcaster and musician Mark Scholz suggested taking the chorus from the song "Time After Time" and put that under the video of people doing patterns. Don produced an opening 30-second montage of the video he had collected of my work over the years, and built a really cool graphic with a clock face to end the show.

We came up with a new name for the presentation: *What Time Do You Have?* The video ran on a television set on the right side of me when I spoke. It took me a good two or three months to get my story broken down into segments timed to end a beat before each patterning video. At first I'd be in the middle of a sentence when the music and video started. It looked and sounded really bad. But we hung in, and in the end I was pretty pleased with the final product. The timing made every show a new challenge to hit those video intros dead-on. I relished that, because it kept me fresh.

The last five-minute segment opened with a question for the audience: "Have you ever wondered what a minute looks like?" Then, in silence, I looked at the clock as it counted sixty seconds.

"What if we took that one minute and multiplied it by five or ten once a week?" I asked. "And what if we shared that time with someone? Because minutes become half hours and then hours. That amount of time we share with someone can make a lifelong impact."

Then I closed with: "What time do you have?"

Bookings were coming in pretty steadily. It came to a point where money was secondary. I just wanted to share my message of hope, community and sharing time with others with as many groups as possible. If we got a request from a small group, I would ask what their budget was and then work around it.

Speakers' bureaus were beginning to show interest, which led to some major out-of-town gigs. I travelled by myself. To make things easier, I flew back and forth from Edmonton the same day as the presentation. It did make for long days but solved countless issues around hotels and attendant care.

When the recession hit in Canada around the mid-2000s, speakers' bureaus took a hit, as well as the entire speaking industry. It was understandable, but I felt the story I had was worth finding every avenue possible to share it. In March 2006, at the Mayfield Inn in Edmonton's west end, I gave the clock presentation to a conference group of eighteen hundred and was given a three-minute standing ovation. I knew there must be ways to get the message out there.

In the fall of 2004, I had seen a story on the CBC news about someone in Nova Scotia who had a dream and shared it with his MLA, who made it happen. It inspired me to call *my* MLA, Gene Zwozdesky, with a dream of my own to get the presentation in front of high school kids and stress the importance of volunteering.

If we want to start making any social change, we need to talk to young people, to provide them with as much information as we can so they will be in a better position to make good decisions. In the early 1980s, people with disabilities were invited into Alberta schools to give presentations on disability. The project proved to be very successful.

Gene was just the man I needed to talk to. In addition to being my MLA, he was the minister of community development and had initiatives to promote volunteering. There was another thing on my side—an Alberta general election was three weeks away.

Gene came through, big time. He quickly arranged a presentation in front of the Wild Rose Foundation, the board that would make the ultimate decision on funding. Using the clock video, I altered the show to talk about the need to share the volunteering concept with high school students. Lucky for me, the board liked what they heard and we hammered out a deal.

My cost was $600 per school, and they agreed to make it an $18,000 deal. My job was to make contact with Edmonton and area high schools, first telling them about the presentation and then seeing if there was any interest.

Gene, a teacher himself who would later go on to be Alberta's minister of education, suggested we aim for CALM classes, short for "career and life management" for high school students. My sister-in-law Betty-Anne was a high school teacher and she helped me get the word out as well as giving me contact information for most principals.

Speaking to high school kids was a whole different deal than talking to volunteers or corporate leaders, and I knew I had to engage them like no other audience before and make it as interactive as possible. I could not talk to them; I had to talk with them.

It was a tough thing to do, but I unplugged the clock video for the last time. Kids were being bombarded with video and I very much wanted to be as personal as I could, to just talk to them without any bells or whistles... or videos.

But that gave me a new issue: How would I be able to describe how a pattern was done without any video?

Like a lot of people, some of my best ideas come to me when I'm in the shower. And, sometime in early 2005, the water gods spoke to me again. Have the students do a pattern. Get a few gym mats and put them on the classroom floor. Ask five volunteers to come up front and instruct them on how to do a pattern.

It was important to get their attention in the first minute of the class, and perhaps my method could be questioned, but I wanted to make a firm statement on how serious I was taking my time with them.

"I don't put up with any horseshit," I opened. "For the next eighty minutes, we are going to respect each other."

I know, I know. Maybe I shouldn't have sworn, but it was nothing they hadn't heard before. I wanted to get down to their level, yet make a point.

We started every class by going up and down the rows of students, asking all to state their names, two things they were hoping to learn from the presentation and what it felt like when they were dancing. Then, the curveball: no first names. Not Jason, Brittany, Keri or Ethan. I wanted Miss Smith, or Mr. Taylor— sending a message to them that I was showing respect.

It was really great to see, because for a good number of students, it was the first time they had put "Miss" or "Mr." in front of their name, and for a few brief seconds after they said it, I could clearly see a look of pride on their faces.

"Now," I said, "I invite everyone to hold your breath for one minute. If you have health concerns, I certainly understand, but those of you who can, please hold your breath for one minute."

I timed sixty seconds on the clock. When it was over, I asked how many people held their breath for thirty seconds, for forty-five seconds, and then finally, for sixty seconds. Then I asked, "How many people here held their breath for eighteen minutes?" and slowly raised my hand.

Some of the students were shocked—I could clearly see it on their faces. Then I explained my gracious entry into the world. I found that to be very effective.

Instead of telling the students what I did for the first five years of my life, I had one of them come to the gym mats, curl up like a ball of wool and say "Mum, Mum, Mum, Mum"—exactly as I'd done.

But the most rewarding part of the class was when I asked five students to come up. The shortest was asked to lie face down on the mat and then I told them how to do a pattern. The rest of the class stood in a semicircle to watch.

It was so very cool to see the kids going through what I had done. I also had a small taste of what my parents must have felt, to see people follow their instructions to help me.

I had the students do the pattern for about a minute, then asked if someone had a calculator. Together, we crunched the numbers: eight patterns a day, for 365 days, for five years. The total was 14,400.

"And I had 5,137 wedgies," was my next line.

My story continued with the bit about my college instructor telling me that I would never work in the media in my life.

I was hard on the students—perhaps too hard. If I heard even the slightest conversation between students, I would stop and asked them what they were talking about, and if they would like to share it with the class. When they declined, I asked them to stand up and apologize to the class for interrupting.

Most students did stand up and say they were sorry. Only a few laughed and thought I was out of line. In those situations, I asked the teacher for permission to ask the student to leave the room. Sometimes, I got mad and it showed; yet, I was trying to teach the respect value, and interrupting someone is very disrespectful. Again, I think I speak from experience. Because of the way I speak, some people are either uncomfortable or impatient around me, so they interrupt me, and start their own conversations. It's frustrating, and very rude.

During the end of the presentation, I asked the students not to call me a hero. Clearly, I am not, and I am uncomfortable when some people call me one. The real heroes, I said, were my parents and the volunteers for their tireless efforts. I outlined the current status of volunteers in Canada and I explained how it scared the heck out of me, that if there was a young person with cerebral palsy today who needed help as I had, he or she might not get it.

I challenged the students to share their time with someone who really needed it.

As the class came to an end, I asked the students not to clap for me. Instead, I asked that they shake my hand—or, if they were so inclined, give me a hug—on their way out of class. I thought that might make our time together a little more personal—and show that it was okay to have physical contact with someone with a disability. And although applause is very nice and appreciative, a handshake, to me, means a great deal more.

Remember that I asked the audience to describe what it felt like when they were dancing? As class was dismissed and students went out the door, I had the teacher hit a song in my CD player: Martha and the Vandellas, "Dancin' in the Streets."

In all, we made thirty visits to high schools in 2005–06. I often made three or four presentations, back to back, on the same day at one school.

The Wild Rose Foundation had a questionnaire for the students to fill out after the presentation, and for the majority, the comments were very flattering.

Near the end of every class, I went around the room again to get feedback from the students. I was not looking for compliments; I wanted to make the presentation the best as I could, and the students were my best critics, so I wanted to hear from them. There were some, of course, who did not like the show—and that is absolutely fair. I respect that not everyone is going to like what I do, and that is their right. But I was focusing on the positive feedback we were getting.

In a perfect world, I could have done the school program free of charge. And, in many cases, I did. But the government deal, in a sense, made me a professional, and I approached it with the respect it deserved.

I struggled about whether or not I should, in fact, charge for my speaking. But several friends often said if I gave it away for free, then it was worthless.

In May 2006, I felt I had come full circle when I was asked

to deliver the keynote address at the World Congress at The Institutes in Philadelphia. Dr. Doman, The Institutes' founder, was in the third row of the lecture theatre—the same lecture theatre in which my parents were taught how to do patterns. As speaker, I was able to thank Dr. Doman. It was moving—and the last speech I gave for a while.

● ● ●

My parents' deaths in 2007–08 put me in a dark place, and I could not give the kind of presentation I needed to. In 2010, Joan suggested I go back and try comedy again, and I did. But I was trying to force the laughs and it just didn't feel right. In fact, on my first night back, I almost wheeled off the stage because I did not have a good sense of where the microphone was. My timing was not there and I knew it wasn't. Then, after one evening onstage, the three men lifting my chair down the steps dropped me halfway down and my head accidentally hit a step. I wasn't hurt badly, although my pride took a rough beating.

I decided I needed more time to heal and to feel the passion again in speaking. I knew it would come, because I kept seeing and hearing the young girl I had spoken with in the corner of a classroom at M.E. Lazerte High School near the end of a class.

"I just found out last week I have cancer. I have leukemia," she said, with her voice cracking. "I have not told many people and a lot of my classmates do not even know this, until now."

There was a long pause.

"But… your story has given me new hope today."

27

Into the Quicksand

Throughout my life I repeatedly told myself I could never be depressed. Never. I have so much to be thankful for. I mean, just look at the love and support I had as a kid, when I needed it the most. I had a wonderful family who did everything for me. Sure, I have a disability, but so do millions of other people. I told myself I had nothing to be depressed about.

Depression, though, was in my genes. My maternal grandfather would sit for months, head down, and not talk to anyone. I tried to fight it as much as I could. There were times—many times, in fact—that I did feel down. But I always had something—a hockey game, an interview, a date with Joan—to get my mind off things... until the summer of 2002.

I told myself I was tired and needed an entire month off to recover from what I had called a gruelling winter in the *Journal* newsroom. I asked my editor, Barb Wilkinson, if I could take four weeks off. There were, after all, five weeks of vacation time owing. Our family cabin in Meota was empty in May. Perfect! So Joan loaded the car and off we went. Our cousins from across the street greeted us the evening we pulled in.

"We're here for a month," I said as I got out of the car.

Meota has over two hundred people. It's quiet and has deep family roots, as my father was born there. Our family had spent summers there since 1972, when Mom and Dad bought a lot with a 16-x-12-foot house built in 1911. There was no indoor plumbing, but the price was right—$1,500. Shortly after, Dad constructed one hell of an outhouse. It wasn't right on the lake; it was on a cliff, behind a road—but had a beautiful view of the lake. When Dad retired in 1986, construction began on our original lot for a beautiful two-storey house overlooking the lake.

I thought a month off at the lake would be great. And for the first week, it was—sleep-ins, not shaving, afternoon naps and so much more great relaxation. Hell, I even got into my wife's favourite soap opera. The second week was good, too, with quality rest and visiting the Tait cousins. But, somewhere in the back of my mind, I was dreading the next two weeks. We had driven everywhere we wanted to go, seen all the people we wanted to. Two words: Now what? I was ready to go back to work, but thought since I had asked for a month off, I'd better use it.

The third week was hell. Pure hell. I woke up every morning, just after four, unable to go back to sleep. The more I tried, the worse it was, creating more anxiety. I didn't realize it at the time, but I was bored. Sure, I had packed my laptop and there was lots I could write. But I was on holiday, right? Sleep was getting to be a bigger issue. One night, I got up five times between 3:00 and 4:00 a.m. I tried turning the clock radio off, shutting the bedroom door tight, turning on the television—anything to help me sleep. I couldn't.

I'd led such a busy and full life, starting with patterning, then school and then working. I had never taken more than two weeks off at a time. My mind started going places I didn't even know existed. I began focusing on my finances and how irresponsible I was with credit. For the first time in my life, I admitted to myself that I was living far beyond my means. I added up the debt in my head: north of $50,000. Plus a mortgage. I had this sick feeling of sinking in quicksand, with no way out. I didn't think about bad things when I was busy, but with nothing to do, I got more and more depressed. I tried not to show it. But Joan knew something was not right.

And sleep—the one thing I could use for an escape—was impossible. I realized long holidays and me are not a good match at all. And that's a good thing. Perhaps I hadn't taught myself how to relax. I found out, the hard way.

We returned to Edmonton and I knew I had a problem. I was exhausted, not having slept in five days. Writing three columns a week—something I did with ease in the past—became a chore. Every sentence was a struggle. My doctor put me on sleeping pills, and that got my strength back, especially in my voice. When I am overtired, I find it really takes an effort to speak. As a consequence, people have an even tougher time understanding me. And for someone who asks questions for a living, I could not let my speech slip. Yet, there was a deeper issue. I was depressed. Very depressed.

But why?

Through experience, I have discovered that some things—for whatever reason—do not have answers.

I caught up on my sleep, but felt terrible mentally. After a weekly staff meeting, editor Barb Wilkinson asked me how I was doing. For the first time in my life, I spoke the words: "I think I'm depressed."

Barb is a wonderful person with a huge heart. "Do yourself a favour," she said. "Tell your doctor."

I swallowed hard and felt that cramp in my throat—the one I get just before I want to cry.

"Okay, I will," I said.

I made another appointment with my doctor, Fraser Armstrong. We'd met in the mid-'70s. I felt comfortable in his west end office, not even a minute's drive from the house I grew up in. Fraser took his time with me, and he had a great understanding of cerebral palsy. I sat in one of the examining rooms when he asked the dreaded question. "Are you depressed?"

"Yes," I said.

He pulled out a pad and wrote out a prescription for an antidepressant.

"This should help, but we need to keep in touch," Fraser said.

The drug helped ease things, but only a little. I was almost afraid to go out the door in the morning, thinking the worst could happen. I couldn't laugh anymore. I could hear the disappointment in Joan's voice.

"One of the reasons I married you was because you made me laugh," she said. "Where has it gone?"

I had no answer. It seemed I had done everything I set out to do. I was married to a wonderful gal. We'd just learned that Darren and AnnaMai were going to make us grandparents. I had a job I absolutely adored, three columns a week about people helping people. It was a workload I thought I handled quite well. I had a home on a ravine, something I had always wanted. At the time, my parents were healthy and happy. I had it all. Made in the shade, man. Yet, there were several days when Joan would leave for a few hours and I would wheel up to the kitchen table and cry uncontrollably.

I went through the motions at the *Journal,* but I knew my heart wasn't in it. My creativity was gone.

In the daytime, when Joan wasn't home, I would take an extra sleeping pill to escape. It became a secret habit that grew to a terrible situation in 2007, the same year my dad died. Joan had picked up a part-time job at Ronald McDonald House, working weekends, twelve hours a day. When she left the condo for her shift one morning just before nine and I knew she wouldn't be home until late that evening, I felt terribly alone. I knew I should visit Mom. I got up and, right before I had breakfast, I wheeled into the den where my little blue sleeping pills were and took four of them, three more than prescribed. It was 10:30 a.m.

I can honestly say I wasn't trying to kill myself. I felt trapped and wanted to get in a vehicle—even a motorcycle—and just... go somewhere. After breakfast I had my regular morning shower and climbed back into bed. I slept until 6:00 p.m., got up, had a bite to eat and waited for Joan to get home. I felt fine—just a little groggy. A few hours later, I took another sleeping pill and had a good night's sleep. No problem, right?

I thought no one would ever know about the amount of pills I had taken. And for the first three days I was fine. But by Thursday, I was in bad shape, shaking so badly I couldn't even steady my head to take a sip from the straw in my morning cup of coffee sitting on the kitchen table. I was anxious and agitated. But the worst was when Joan and I made the hour drive from Edmonton to Camrose for the opening of a new arena. I was so shaky I could barely wheel myself backwards in my chair. In fact, Joan had to push me to get off the elevator, a task I normally could do with ease.

The next day, I came clean with Joan and admitted how many sleeping pills I took. She had every reason to be angry and let me have it pretty good. I deserved it. When I saw the hurt and concern in my wife's eyes, I felt even worse, especially knowing I brought the entire situation upon myself. A few days after I admitted I took extra pills, Darren wheeled me into the den at home. He knelt down, tears suddenly streaming down his face.

"You are my hero," he said, and then started to sob. "How can you do this to your health?"

Now we were both crying.

After my lecture, Joan told me I needed to get to my doctor for help. I went back to Dr. Armstrong and told him what I had done.

"Are you disappointed in me?" I asked.

"Disappointed? No," Fraser said. "But very concerned."

He prescribed a dose of sleeping pills so I could wean myself off them.

I had to do some real soul searching and frankly ask myself why I was so unhappy. Maybe unhappy is the wrong word. My life had changed. I wasn't doing a very good job of accepting the change. I wasn't being fair to my wife, the one person who was keeping me afloat. She stood beside me throughout my dark journey and was firm when I screwed up, but more loving than I can ever express.

Turning the corner took me years, and I was surprised at how slow the process was before I started feeling good again. In 2010, I stopped taking medication. The first thing I noticed was an increase in my creativity when I was writing. Slowly, I found myself wanting to do more. I regained confidence in myself.

I would not have made the progress I did without the wonderful support of my wife and son. I can never tell Joan how much she did for me. And to thank her, I vow to keep myself as busy as I possibly can. Joan and Darren, you saved me.

28

Exit, Stage Left

The summer of 2007 was warm and sunny in Edmonton. But there was a perfect storm brewing in my head and heart.

I missed my parents so much. Mom was in a seniors' locked-down facility, her memories tucked away somewhere, conversations limited to a few sentences on the days she remembered who I was. Dad had passed, something I'd tried to prepare myself for, but now in reality I couldn't have imagined. I had phoned him every day—sometimes three or four times. Without those calls, I felt lost.

"Dial the number," a friend suggested. "Even if someone answers, hang up. But dial your dad's number."

I tried, and for a few moments, it felt good. Then the sadness washed over me like a wave.

My work was slipping, too. I fought to write every sentence. I was getting names and statistics wrong. Sports editor Bob Boehm had every reason to be angry with me—and was. Deep down I knew I should take some time off, but another part of me said that was the easy thing to do and I had to keep working. Besides, it was baseball season and I was covering the Edmonton Cracker-Cats and got to spend eight hours a day in the sunshine at a baseball park and get paid for it. How good was that?

Still, I was making mistakes in the raw copy I was sending to the sports desk—especially names. It was a big issue, because my copy was coming in so close to deadline and the editors didn't have time to double-check names. When your mistakes end up in the paper, the desk has a major problem, and so do you. To this day, I don't know why it happened. I doubled-checked names before filing my copy, or thought I did. But the mistakes kept coming.

To make matters worse, the entire newspaper industry was being forced by technology into massive change in an effort to stay viable. When the Internet lit up things in the mid-1990s, we heard rumblings that change was inevitable, but no one anticipated what that would mean, or that it would come so quickly, because in some ways the new approach was great.

Email changed the way I interviewed people and it took me a while to adjust. I never liked going into an interview with a set of questions. I think it puts a reporter in a box—because, if someone says something really interesting but unexpected, that's a door you should go through. With a pre-set agenda, you might leave it closed. I've always viewed an interview as a conversation. Many times I would hide my tape recorder under a seat so the person would just talk to me. I like to see the expression on someone's face after they answer a question, or whether they sigh, or tap their middle finger when they talk. You can't capture that in email.

But email does other things. In my case, my questions were read and people could really understand them, rather than listening to my voice, which some found difficult to understand. Email interviews put everyone on an equal playing field, and no one can ever claim misquotation. Mind you, I still preferred crafting a story by listening to the tape, rewinding it when I had to, and taking my time. But those damned early Internet deadlines and the emphasis on getting everything onto the paper's web page instantly, if not sooner, often made that impossible.

Pre-Internet, I could attend a breakfast meeting, get back to the office around 9:30, have coffee, go over my notes carefully and really take my time crafting a story for filing by around 1:30 p.m. In the web world, with the paper screaming for copy, I would rush home, fire off a hasty 300-word story, then rewrite a longer version for the newspaper to be published early the next morning. As a newspaper guy, it galled. The web was beating me to my own story by sixteen hours.

Nobody in the executive suite is ever likely to admit it, but with the sheer volume of web and print edition copy coming to the news desk and forcing early deadlines, the quality often suffered. There was just no time to polish the work.

How's this for irony? The very technology that helped me do my job was the thing that cost my early exit from the *Journal*.

A reality check came in late February 2008, when Bob Boehm called me into his office and told me he was taking me off covering the Alberta Junior Hockey League playoffs. My mistakes were just too big. The news desk could no longer trust the information I was providing.

I was frustrated, and a little angry. So many things in my life were changing that I couldn't focus on the one beat I had wanted all my life. It was also hard on the ego. The only saving grace was that I was still at the games, mentoring a great young reporter, Chris O'Leary, and introducing him to players and coaches—and I had my blog on the *Journal*'s website, which gave me an outlet for my opinions on the games.

Blogging was great fun. I'd always wanted to produce video and loved working with sound. Now I could record video interviews with the camera on my laptop, edit the piece down to 90 seconds, and fire it onto the web. But I was only delaying the inevitable.

The newspaper industry was starting to gasp for air. The *Journal* was offering voluntary buyouts in the fall of 2010 and the sports department took a few big hits. Bob Boehm, who used to sit across from me in the late 1980s and opened my mail, decided to leave as sports editor. Veteran reporter John Korobaniak put his hand up, too, and left the paper. This was further motivation for me to be more accountable so I wouldn't get the tap on the shoulder.

But in the fall of 2011, I was given a great assignment. *Journal* sports editor Paul Cashman was having staffing issues and couldn't cover Edmonton Oil Kings' home games on a regular basis. He called me in October and asked if I could write another column, this one specifically on the Oil Kings. This was perfectly made to measure for me: I still got to be around, and covering, junior hockey—but it didn't have the looming pressure of writing on deadline. I made the column a place where we told stories of the players and staff who were the bloodline of the Oil Kings. Things got even better in the spring of 2012 when I was asked to cover the Alberta Junior Hockey League playoffs. Writing game stories. On deadline. I was finally back in the saddle.

Maybe I was naïve about just how bad a financial shape the *Journal* was in. Perhaps I ignored it. The *Journal* announced in May that the Sunday paper would no longer be published.

Without a Sunday paper, my community column needed a new home, since it ran on that day. I pitched a move to Mondays and to make it upbeat, with good news, trying to give folks a good start to their week. I also shared my desire to write two or three more columns a week. Honestly, columns were easier for me to write because they were my insights and opinions. Sure, quotes from people would flush out the argument more, but they weren't essential as in a news story. A column challenges one's writing style. I thought if I had a strong perspective on an issue, dabbled a little writing pizzazz and sprinkled it with emotion, a column might emerge.

In June, I had a new gig: one city column and three sports pieces a week, thanks to the new sports editor, Craig Ellingson. I found myself interviewing old acquaintances like Glen Sather and Theo Fleury, but also making new contacts in the Edmonton sports scene.

In mid-July, *Journal* sports columnist John MacKinnon was on holidays when the Edmonton Eskimos were playing at home. I would never trample on MacKinnon's toes and wasn't taking aim at his job. But I knew we weren't going to have a columnist at the Eskimo game, so I asked if I could write the column. Who knew it would be my farewell piece?

Over the years, the *Journal* had its fair share of farewell parties in the newsroom. Many, many talented, wonderful people lost their jobs, but I never thought it would happen to me. Maybe my ego got in the way, but I just thought getting rid of the guy in the wheelchair who wrote about good community endeavours might be bad optics for the paper. I was naïve.

There had been rumblings in the early summer that twenty-five newsroom staffers would be let go. I told Joan, but assured her I wasn't going anywhere. I was writing more, getting good response and felt as if I had a new lease on my career.

On July 18, 2011, an all-newsroom email from editor-in-chief Lucinda Chodan informed us that cuts would be announced the next day and some staff might be called into her office.

It won't be me, I told myself. In fact, I thought, I'll call Lucinda myself to set up a meeting and talk about how I could have a bigger role to help with things.

We met the next morning in a room at our condo complex. When I saw her pull up in her red car, I knew my life was about to change. She had company—the *Journal*'s vice-president of human resources, Gail Matheson. Sticking out from her purse was a *Journal* envelope with CAMERON TAIT typed on the front.

"As you know, Cam, we've had to make some hard decisions," Lucinda said. "I am very sorry to tell you we are letting you go."

I looked to the ceiling in disbelief. I wanted to know why. I wanted to slam my fist against the wall. I wanted to cry. I wanted my job back.

Lucinda went on to say that my last day of work would be August 31. With my years of service, I would get $120,000 in severance pay.

"We'd like you to write a freelance column for us," Lucinda said. "I think we pay about $200 a column."

I swallowed hard. "I'd be honoured to," I replied.

And then, like that, the meeting was over.

I have wheeled myself down the hall of our condo building to our unit thousands of times. On that day, it seemed a thousand kilometres long. I dreaded telling Joan. The feeling of being a failure was slowly washing over me. How would I support my family?

I went in with the *Journal* letter in my hand. Joan was on the couch. When she saw it, she gasped and covered her mouth. We both sat in silence for a minute. We were in shock.

"You lost your job?" she asked.

She came over and held me for several minutes while my head was swimming. I remembered that summer of 2002 when I took a month off, became extremely bored and then even more depressed. No matter what, I thought as I gritted my teeth, I had to keep moving... keep going. Otherwise I would be in huge trouble.

Suddenly I felt the need to reach out to my friends. After a few hours of letting the news sink in, I called Terry Jones, a long-time columnist at the *Edmonton Sun*. Terry was with the *Journal* when I started freelancing and has always been very supportive. I needed to say thank you.

It was so hard to say I lost my job—and it never got easier. I sent out an email to about fifty friends with my news. Many people responded within a half hour, all truly supportive.

Long-time radio executive Marty Forbes emailed me. Marty was writing a freelance column for the *Edmonton Sun* and asked if he could give the *Sun* publisher my number. I said yes because I felt it was important for me to keep going, but I went one step further. I emailed *Sun* editor Steve Serviss and asked to meet for coffee, and we did—the very next day, in fact, in the same room as my meeting with the *Journal*.

Steve said he didn't have anything full-time but would like me to write one column a week at $250 per column. Hell of a deal, I thought. Fifty bucks more than what the *Journal* had offered. A few days later, I had lunch with Edmonton Oilers president Patrick LaForge and talked about a part-time job writing for the Oilers. Then I emailed Lucinda Chodan and told her I wouldn't be writing a column for the *Journal*. As it turned out, I was wrong. A double-check of my severance package showed that, had I taken the *Sun* deal, I could have lost my *Journal* severance money.

I called *Journal* sports editor Craig Ellingson and asked if I could, after all, write the weekly column I was originally offered. There was an uncomfortable silence. Since I had initially turned it down, he wasn't sure. He'd have to talk to Lucinda and call me back.

I sweated out the wait for the verdict. Had I done a number on myself? What if the *Journal* said no? How stupid was I?

Craig called back within five minutes. No problem, he said. I would start writing a weekly column on a freelance basis in September 2012. It was merely a stay of execution.

I knew that I was gonzo at the end of August. It was hard giving the *Journal* my best effort, knowing I would never be covering the same events again. Damn hard. Somehow, though, I did it.

My last day as a full-time reporter was August 31. I went in for a farewell get-together with the other staff who were let go. It was very weird.

I was 54 years old. The newspaper business, as I'd known it, was dying. I'd had a wonderful run, first as a freelance writer in 1979, and then as a staffer from 1985. I wanted to be treated like anyone else. And I was.

Now, remember, I got the news about being let go six days after I wrote a column on an Edmonton Eskimo game. Jim Taylor had a great line: "First, they give you a column on the Eskimos and then they punt you. Geez, that's one hell of a send-off."

But one of life's great truisms is that if you're lucky enough to have good friends, they will be there for you when you've got troubles. My friends have proven it over and over again. A few weeks before my last day at the *Journal*, Cam McGinness took me for an early morning round at the Edmonton Country Club. Kevin Shaigec joined our foursome. When he heard of my pending unemployment, he asked if I was working on my autobiography, which had been an on-again, off-again project for about twenty years.

"No," I said. "But it's certainly back on my to-do list now that I've got time on my hands."

Kevin owned Challenge Insurance in Edmonton. "If you need an office, I have one for you." he said.

That was music to my ears. That month off in 2002, and the resulting deep depression, had taught me what could happen when I had nothing to do. The book would provide the project, and now Kevin was providing the place to do it. The rest was up to me.

I have been known to procrastinate somewhat. (Just ask Jim Taylor.) I need firm deadlines to get things done. A local book publisher said they would be interested in looking at my manuscript, and informed me that a biography should run about 80,000 words. A word count on what I'd already written confirmed that

I was about 52,000 words short—and I had seven weeks to meet their deadline. Perfect.

Going into the Challenge Insurance office was great. I got into a routine and the work got done. Then one day when the words just weren't coming, I heard Kevin mention that he wanted a new radio commercial written for the agency. Wait a minute. I loved to write radio commercials! So I did—and the next day it was on the radio. And then I got back to the book.

I delivered close to 70,000 words to the publisher at the end of October. Five months later, I got a "Dear Cam" email from the publisher saying they weren't interested. But, at least it was written—and I had a new job. Kevin made me special projects advisor with Challenge Insurance. I handle their social media and radio commercials, and I've designed a new speaking presentation for high school students.

I was back in the communication game.

29
......

Do You Hear the Drums, Fernando?

The quickest way to learn to truly appreciate what you have is to wake up one morning and discover that you could lose it all. My wake-up call came in late spring 2013, when the Alberta government decided to make sweeping changes in its home care system.

In our condominium, we had known for a couple of months that something was coming, and that it might be scary and could put our existing care system in jeopardy. When the word of impending change came down, the message wasn't what you'd call subtle. For all existing programs, such as the one in use in our condominium, the committee had to submit a proposal for a new contract. And, oh, by the way, if any of us went to our MLA or—for shame—the media, our proposal would be disqualified.

Can you say "gag order"?

We played by the rules, hoping and praying our proposal would be chosen. If it weren't, things would drastically change for all fourteen of us who lived in the condo complex and used our home care services.

We had a very unique situation. We administered the program ourselves and had a direct say in our daily care. The majority of our staff has been with us for ten years or more. And because of that, they know our wants and needs extremely well. In my case, the staff member who comes in to help me get up in the morning knows how to wheel me into the shower, and knows the amount of milk I like in my coffee. That's priceless.

If a new contract was awarded, we couldn't keep the staff we had. A new company would come in with their own people. What was more, the government didn't communicate with us at all. They just said it wasn't good enough anymore. They couldn't specifically tell us why—just that it wasn't working.

I was scared. Very scared. Joan and I had a lovely home, but more importantly, we had help for my personal care. If new people came in, would they be any good? Would that mean we would have to move from the condo—and, if so, where would we go? And, on the far wall of my brain was the thought that I might have to move into a nursing home. I cringed at the thought. Our grandson, Nicholas, was 10 years old and lived five minutes away from us. Having Nicholas over was very precious, and he was at the age where I could babysit him if Joan had to go out for a few minutes. We played video games, watched television and even made rude body sounds only males can make—and then laughed wildly. How could I do those kinds of things in a nursing home?

We were hoping those fears would never be faced. But in our hearts we knew otherwise. Sure enough, Larry Pempeit, president of Creekside Support Services, called an emergency meeting on the last Sunday in May and told the home care users the government had rejected our proposal. We met in a common room just off the lobby in our condo and sifted through many emotions.

Do You Hear the Drums, Fernando?

We were mad, dammit. How could anyone come into our homes and dismantle a home care program that started in 1997—a program that ran like clockwork?

We were scared, not only for our own personal care—but also the future of the wonderful staff we had. They had families. They didn't deserve to be laid off by some bonehead decision.

We were frustrated. By having a self-directed care program, we had control of our own lives. That, by itself, gave us dignity.

So there was only one thing left to do: fight like hell.

I was struck by the calm confidence in the meeting as we divided up the work to do. Larry gave us the green light to start making some noise with mainstream media. I offered to call my reporter friends in Edmonton.

Surprisingly, though, the new way of telling a message—social media—turned out to be one of the most valuable items in our tool belt. It was amazing. Marty Forbes, a long-time radio executive, had inspired me to start a blog in April, two months before we got word on our home care contract. Now we decided the blog might be a good place to tell our story on a daily basis. Heidi Janz, who hadn't let her cerebral palsy stop her from getting her Ph.D. in C.O.D. and becoming a brilliant writer and playwright, offered to set up a Facebook page to share our story and gain support.

We had to work fast. Our contract was set to expire at the end of July. We went back to our suites, fired up our computers and buckled up for the ride of our lives.

I introduced our challenge the next day on my morning blog post called Cam 'n Eggs. I got rather personal, describing how I get help from our staff with showering, shaving and the other s-word in the morning. Maybe I went a tad overboard, but I wanted to tell the story of the importance of having personal care in our own home.

After two days, the blog really gained momentum and other people with disabilities were sharing their stories with me. I posted every one, word for word—and I was thrilled with the response because it showed readers this wasn't just about me. I kept hearing my editors when I was writing for the *Journal*. Something like: "The more voices, the better." We had plenty of voices. The government was planning to cancel a total of three user-driven home care programs—ours at Creekside, Abbey Road Co-op and Art Space Co-op. We sent out emails to residents at the other two, asking them to share their thoughts and fears. And we had Heidi, who wasn't just an advocate. Heidi was a force.

She got Facebook rolling and we shared the blog links on the page. She also started an online petition against Alberta premier Alison Redford. A week went by and we felt great momentum. I called my friends at the *Journal* and the *Sun* as well as all three television stations. The story was slowly getting out there.

Eight days after we first met as a group, Heidi and I were riding the same Disabled Adult Transit System vehicle on our way to work when I posed a question: "What if we wrote a letter to the premier on the blog and asked her over for coffee?"

Heidi smiled widely. "Go for it," she said.

By noon I posted the blog asking Redford for coffee, with a little dig at the end, offering to buy the coffee since the provincial government appeared to be broke.

The next day, all hell broke loose. Three home care officials met with all of the Creekside users just after four in the afternoon to tell us how our care was going to change. We fought back and said we were not going to accept their plan. They were not very prepared, and could not give us concrete answers on how their proposed system would work, only a vague "the level of care will not change."

How could they guarantee that? How could they even say it? One of our big concerns was losing our 24-hour on-site staff. Under the new regime, an outside agency would send workers to the condo who would help us, and then leave. No on-site staff office. No consistency. Just a bunch of come-and-go drop-ins. If somebody using our services spilled a glass of water and called for help, our calls could have very well been answered by someone on the other side of Edmonton, half an hour away. They might have to finish helping someone else before climbing into their vehicle to drive to our condo. A spilled glass of water is one thing. But what if someone had an accident in the washroom? Or fell? Or...? Waiting half an hour for help could be very dangerous.

Just as I felt my heart rate and blood pressure rise, the home care officials revealed something that was astounding. Like every condo building, every suite is owned. So how do you think every condo board owner would feel about giving several keys to the front door of the building to home care workers from an outside agency so they can come in and help people? Our condo board—a separate entity from the home care program—would never agree to such an idea.

"Oh," one of the government officials said. "We didn't realize that."

"Nice to see you did your homework," I piped up. And then I got mad.

"You know what you're doing here? You're killing our spirit with your decision. And what the hell do I tell my grandson when Grampa has to go into a nursing home because of the government. Shame on you. Shame on you!"

I was beyond angry. I was furious that the government hadn't done more homework about our program; furious that they were making wholesale changes to our program with absolutely no consultation with us; furious that these people allegedly in charge of how we would conduct our lives couldn't even provide any answers as to what the new system would provide or how it would work.

I was flirting with apoplexy when gale-force Heidi played her ace.

She introduced her good friend, Reverend Shafer Parker, who had come to the meeting to help translate her speech, which her cerebral palsy sometimes makes difficult to understand. Then she smiled sweetly and asked Reverend Parker to give an outsider's view of the situation.

"I find it appalling," Shafer said without a second's thought. "What you're about to do in the homes of people here is absolutely appalling."

We were now better than an hour into the meeting and spinning our tires. Government officials were saying our care wasn't going to change, even though, fundamentally, we knew it would. We were saying we weren't going to accept it. Larry suggested we adjourn. Good thing, because we were getting dizzy.

I wheeled into my suite just before 5:30 p.m. to check my email, and there it was—a message sent an hour earlier by Neala Barton, director of communications for Premier Redford. The premier had agreed to meet us for coffee in five days. Suddenly, I felt the game change. I printed it off and grabbed the phone to call Larry two floors above me.

"Got any Scotch up there?" I asked. "I have some news."

I went up and shared the latest development with him. We talked and had a brief discussion of how we should go about our meeting.

"I have some hope now," Larry said as I opened the door to leave. "Haven't had that for a while."

We felt a movement growing. Our online petition had close to fifteen hundred names. The blog was posted on Facebook and being sent out on emails. We couldn't let up.

The next day, we met with our MLA, Rachel Notley of the NDP. Following the meeting, we met privately and I shared the news of the upcoming meeting with Redford. I thought Heidi was going to jump out of her power wheelchair.

"Wanna come?" I asked.

"Yes, I do," she said.

The days leading up to the meeting seemed to drag into years. We wanted to keep it quiet, but the word was slowly getting out in our condo.

Our meeting was at 10:00 a.m. June 16—Father's Day. I had staff come in to assist me with my shower at six o'clock. Okay, I might be getting too personal here when I say that I brush my teeth in the shower. My personal care attendant puts toothpaste on my toothbrush and hands it to me while I sit on a plastic shower chair. But maybe the stress of the situation was getting to everyone. The staff member accidentally took medicated ointment from the bathroom drawer and layered it on my toothbrush. Tasted like hell, and I almost threw up, but I suppose I had great breath to meet the premier.

Heidi and I met in the condo lobby for our nine o'clock pick-up. Heidi's church congregation, Zion Baptist Community Church, just a few blocks west, was praying for our meeting. The wife of Zion's senior pastor came along with us to translate for Heidi.

We met Larry at the Alberta legislature and were taken to a meeting room to await Premier Redford. The silence in the room signalled the importance of what we were about to do. Redford and a few aides came into the room at 10:05 with then Human Services minister Dave Hancock.

Larry carried the torch. He told the group about the Creekside history, its success and how we were completely blindsided by the changes.

Redford clearly had no idea what the Alberta Health Services bureaucrats were doing. Neither did Hancock. And as Larry calmly—very calmly—explained what the ramifications were if the changes were implemented, I saw a huge tear drop from Redford's left eye. She quickly wiped it away and got on with business.

She said, "I want to make sure I understand this" several times. Aides quickly made notes as Larry continued talking. We only had thirty minutes and needed to have every one of them count. Time flew by.

Redford got up to leave. "We have work to do," she said. "We don't have much time."

Heidi and I were waiting for our ride home at the east entrance of the legislature. It was raining lightly outside, but I had a bright ray of hope inside.

"How do you think we did?" Heidi asked.

"I think we hit one out of the park," I replied. And I did. We didn't whine. We didn't yell and scream or jump up and down and throw things. We simply told our story, nothing more.

We went back to telling our story—updating Facebook, sending out tweets linked to blog posts and asking people to sign the online petition. We had over 2,200 names, but wanted more.

So we hunkered down and told more stories. June 20 was a Tuesday, and I went to my Challenge Insurance office. Neala Barton from the premier's communications office sent me an email just before 12:30 p.m. and asked me to phone her. My fingers couldn't dial fast enough.

"I have something to tell you," Neala began. "There's a press release going out in half an hour. The decision has been reversed, and there will be no changes at your condo and the two other programs in Edmonton. Your meeting made an impact."

Speechless, I started to cry.

"Can I hug you?" I somehow managed.

Neala laughed. "I'm glad we could help."

We said our goodbyes and I dropped the receiver on my desk.

Incredible relief swept over my body. I called Larry and Joy Gossell, the coordinator of our program. We all cried together.

We'd fought, and we'd won. The battles will go on, but I have faith that we planted the seed for a new awareness in the halls of power. We have a new premier now, Jim Prentice, and in July 2014 I was appointed to the Premier's Council of Status of Persons with

Disabilities in Alberta—a two-year term. It was a huge honour for me on many levels, perhaps the biggest being that the council was started by my dear friend Gary McPherson in 1988. Gary was a force for people with disabilities and, since his 2010 death at age 63, disability issues haven't been talked about much. Old friend, I hope I do you proud.

Going in our front door that afternoon had a whole new meaning. I was home—and I knew I would continue to be safe there. Nicholas met me at the door, as he always did, with a huge smile on his face. "Papa, I won at school today. We had a paper airplane throwing contest outside, and I threw it the furthest. I won, Papa. I won."

I hugged him even tighter than usual.

"Me, too, Nic," I said. "Me, too."

Five days later we had a barbecue with all our members and staff. We gathered in a semi-circle in front of the condo and burned all the letters from the government informing us our home care was changing.

We had won our personal battle, but that was just part of it. We had proved to the able-bodied community—and to ourselves—that we could and would fight for our rights and beliefs, that our lives were sewn into the social fabric with everyone else, that we could use the tools of Facebook and Twitter and text and blog to make our voices heard, and that—should battle lines need to be drawn again—we would be at the front, not in the commissary.

It's amazing how we're placed in different situations in different phases of our lives. I wouldn't have been able to bang the drum as loudly as I did if I was still working at the *Journal*. But now I could spread my wings and tell the story.

The power of social media absolutely stunned me. We had kept asking people to sign our online petition, and by the time we got word the decision was reversed, we had over 2,500 names.

It was the greatest team victory I had ever been a part of. Not only did we keep our home care, we made a very profound statement about people with disabilities living independently, and in doing so, gained a new level of respect by many. You can't put a price on that.

Epilogue

'm sitting here now, suddenly 56 years old. Yesterday I was 20. What happened?

This afternoon, the grandson I helped to take his first steps what seems like a couple of weeks ago scored two goals in his pee wee hockey game—the tying goal in the third period and the winner in overtime. If I blink, will he be an Oiler?

My wonderful wife is sitting here with me, which makes every day brighter and ranks atop my list of blessings.

In the back of my mind, there's this glorious, nagging little itch reminding me that I've got a column to write for my new twice-a-week gig—Tait on 8—for my new employers, the *Edmonton Sun*. Ah, Rimmer, thank you for the encouragement and the help, all those years ago. I'll try to make you proud.

True, my life has had its setbacks and things I'd go back and change if I could—but hasn't everyone's? On balance, I can look skyward and give a fervent "Thank you!" for so many things and so many people that I would need another volume just to list them.

It amazes me to think about it.

Still doing comedy, 22 years after I gave it my first shot.

If my mom and dad had been less determined to instill in me the refusal to see my disability as a deterrent to living a full life, would I have golfed with Gretzky, swum a mile, gone parasailing, or had the nerve to take the stage at Yuk Yuk's?

How much easier and simpler would it have been for the neighbours who committed themselves to the patterning sessions to limit their compassion to sympathetic nods and get on with their own busy lives?

In the often-frantic world of media, the *Journal* brass and editors logically could have looked at the funny-voiced kid in the wheelchair who had this crazy dream of being a reporter, mentally run down the long list of potential hurdles and inconveniences, and brushed him off with "Sorry, kid. Next!" But they didn't. They gave me my chance and, better yet, demanded that I prove them right by producing or wheel my butt to Manpower.

And that's the point, really. People with disabilities aren't looking for concessions. They're looking for a chance.

Epilogue

To all of you who gave mine to me, and to those who will one day give that same chance to others, thank you. It's been a wonderful ride.

About the Authors

Cam Tait worked as a reporter for the *Edmonton Journal* for over thirty years, interviewing Wayne Gretzky, Stevie Wonder, James Brady and others. He now writes for the *Edmonton Sun*. He has two honorary degrees and much insight on the subject of which drinking straws go best with which adult beverages. He lives in Edmonton with his wife Joan. This is his first book.

Jim Taylor has produced some 7,500 sports columns, three times as many radio shows and fifteen books. His passion has earned him membership in the CFL and BC Sports Halls of Fame and a lifetime achievement award from Sports Media Canada. He is the co-author of *Goin' Deep: The Life and Times of a CFL Quarterback* with Matt Dunigan and *"Hello, Sweetheart? Gimmie Rewrite!": My Life in the Wonderful World of Sports*. He lives in Shawnigan Lake, BC.